Anne Frank and After

Anne Frank and After

Dutch Holocaust Literature in Historical Perspective

DICK VAN GALEN LAST
ROLF WOLFSWINKEL

AMSTERDAM UNIVERSITY PRESS

Cover design: Marianne Wijsbeek, Loosdrecht
Typesetting: JAPES, Jaap Prummel, Amsterdam

© Amsterdam University Press, Amsterdam, 1996

ISBN 90 5356 182 x (hardbound)
ISBN 90 5356 177 3 (paperback)

Table of Contents

Acknowledgments 7

Introduction: 'Statistics Don't Bleed' 9

Chapter I: Dutch Jewry before 10 May 1940 15

Chapter II: From Aryan Declaration to Yellow Star: the Antechamber of Death 33

Chapter III: Deportation or into Hiding 53

Chapter IV: The Transit Camps 75

Chapter V: The Railroad of No Return 91

Chapter VI: The Paradox of Silence: Survivors and Losers 121

Chapter VII: The Epilogue 147

Notes 155

Chronology 165

Short Biographies 167

Bibliography 173

Sources 179

Index 181

Acknowledgments

The idea for this book first came up in 1993, during a sabbatical spent in Ann Arbor, MI, lecturing on the subject of Dutch Holocaust literature at the University of Michigan. The lecturer in Dutch Studies in the Department of Germanic Studies, Ton Broos, had issued an invitation to come over from Cape Town, South Africa, to present a series of lectures. The response to that course was such that a decision was taken to do further research and write a book on the same subject.

In writing this book we have had the help of a number of people. It is only right that their names are recorded here as a small expression of our gratitude: Jacob Boas, Martijn van Hennik, Karel Margry, Henry Mason, Guus Meershoek, Bob Moore, Jos Scheren, Coen Stuldreher, Odette Vlessing, all of whom read the manuscript, or parts of it, in its pre-publication phase and commented or added their valuable knowledge. Lesly Marx in Cape Town took the trouble to check the complete text for grammatical errors and idiomatic faux-pas.

Many thanks are also due to Royden Yates (University of Cape Town) and Gerard Aalders (Dutch State Institute for War Documentation) for facilitating all the e-mail messages between Amsterdam and Cape Town.

It goes without saying that the responsibility for the choice of quotations rests completely with the authors.

Amsterdam/Cape Town

Dick van Galen Last
Rolf Wolfswinkel

Introduction

'Statistics Don't Bleed'

On the 1st September 1939 the German Army invaded Poland, and the Second World War began. In the spring of 1940, after successfully concluding his campaign in Eastern Europe with the occupation of Poland, Hitler started his offensive in the West. In April he occupied Denmark and Norway, and on 10 May the German armies attacked Holland, Belgium and France at the same time.

It was a rude awakening for a country that had not been involved in a European war since the days of Napoleon and believed implicitly in its policy of neutrality and impartiality. During the First World War it had proved a very advantageous policy as well. This time it was not to be. Queen Wilhelmina and her government fled to London, and on 15 May the Dutch army capitulated. Five long years of occupation by Nazi Germany followed. Those five years have left deep wounds in the lives of many Dutch people. Almost 100,000 fatalities among soldiers, underground resistance fighters and civilians, the hardships of the Japanese prisoner-of-war camps, the forced employment of many men in Germany and the 'hungerwinter' of 1944-1945 are all etched into the collective memory of many Dutch men and women.

But all the hardships suffered in Holland pale in comparison with the fate of the Dutch Jews. In 1965 the Jewish historian Jacques Presser published his extensive study about the persecution of Dutch Jewry, *Ondergang* (translated into English as *Ashes in the Wind*; American title: *The Destruction of the Dutch Jews*). He began his introduction with these telling sentences:

> This book tells the history of murder – of murder on a scale never known before, with malice aforethought and in cold blood. The murderers were Germans, their victims Jews... (Presser, 1969:1)

Unrelated to any wartime or military imperative, the German occupier took the first measures against the Jews of Holland as early as 1940. Step by step they were first identified, isolated and then deported. During 1942 and 1943 virtually all Jews who had been unable to get away or to go into hiding were transported to the concentration camps and the gas chambers in Eastern Europe. More than 100,000 of them never returned.

Fifty years later Holland still struggles with that past. One might say that the crime of the Nazis has not only been the murder of the Jews, but also creating the so-called survivors' guilt. This is the feeling among survivors that they had not done enough to try and save their families; the nightmare that the second generation only lives to replace the others, that they are only surrogates, that those others, the murdered ones, deserved life more than they themselves. Holland is different from other countries occupied by the Nazis in that it is very aware of how much it has been found wanting. How was it possible that the long tradition of tolerance and forbearance was discarded so easily? How was it possible that countrymen were expelled who had lived peacefully in the same country for generations?

Part of the explanation might be inspired by a calvinistic need for guilt. Holland is a country in many ways characterised by a culture of guilt.

But there are also objective, or rather historical, reasons for this feeling. In 1945 three out of four Dutch Jews were dead. Nowhere else, except in Eastern Europe, was the percentage that high. Not without reason could Adolf Eichmann, the man responsible for the execution of the *Endlösung* (Final Solution), report to his superiors in Berlin that the deportations from Holland 'were a pleasure to behold'.

This book will confine itself to Holland, although the persecution of Dutch Jewry is part of a greater European scheme. Hitler had announced in his speech before the Reichstag in January 1939 that all European Jews faced destruction. The outbreak of the Second World War in September of that same year made it possible to put that threat into practice. Six million Jews would become victims: two out of three European Jews were murdered. The project very nearly succeeded, and in many places in Eastern Europe it did succeed entirely. Louis de Jong, who minutely described the history of Holland during the years of occupation, called the Holocaust *the central event of every European Jew who is one of the survivors.*

Reading about this disaster, many people ask today: 'How was this possible?!' It seems inconceivable at the end of the twentieth century in Europe. But it was inconceivable even then, to Jews and non-Jews alike. That is part of the explanation of why it did happen.

                                        *

Here the story of this catastrophe is told on the basis of testimonies from Dutch literature. The *Diary of Anne Frank* is the best-known of these testimonies; it is the most widely read book in the world, after *The Bible*. We also make frequent use of the thorough studies of three of Holland's most important historians of the Jewish catastrophe: Abel Herzberg (1893-1989), Jacques Presser (1899-1970) and Louis de Jong (b. 1914). All three suffered personal losses in the Shoah, and all three have tried to distance themselves from these experiences in their work. Herzberg's aim, for example, was not only to control his emotions, but to transcend them. That was, to him, the only sensible response to the persecutions. Herzberg was taken to several concentration camps, but survived. Presser survived the war by going into hiding, but lost his young wife Dé. He also wrote novellas, crime novels and poetry. De Jong escaped to England early in the war, but lost almost his entire family.

Where these works have not been translated, we have translated quotations into English. We will indicate this in the text by adding 'own translation' between parentheses. As far as possible, however, we have tried to use sources which have already been translated and are therefore accessible for further reading.

We made a conscious decision to tell the story of this black chapter in the history of Holland on the basis of personal testimonies. The switching from a microlevel – the personal testimonies – via a middle level – the history of the persecution of the Jews in Holland – to a macrolevel – the history of the Final Solution – should not confuse the reader. We believe that the nature of the Holocaust is too extensive and too complex to understand comprehensively, and we agree with Arthur Koestler who wrote already in 1944 that small fragments of that complicated historical process can allow for a better perspective on the catastrophe:

> Distance in space and time degrades intensity of awareness. So does magnitude. Seventeen is a figure which I know intimately like a friend; fifty billions is just a sound. A dog run over by a car upsets our emotional balance and digestion; three million Jews killed in Poland cause but a moderate uneasiness. Statistics don't bleed; it is the detail which counts. We are unable to embrace the total process with our awareness; we can only focus on little lumps of reality. (Koestler, 1985:97)

In addition, we have observed a clear change of direction in recent historiography: interest has moved from the collective history to the individual history of persons and their direct environment. In 1995 – 50 years after the liberation – more personal memoirs and local studies about the Second World War and the Holocaust were published in Holland than scholarly studies. It is our intention to integrate these individual voices into the history of the anti-Jewish policies of the Nazis. We will give an individual voice not only to the victims but, where possible, also to the bystanders and the perpetrators.

We were very much aware that the selection of our sources would of necessity be arbitrary: this was unavoidable considering the vast quantity of survivor memoirs. As much as possible we preferred to use 'ego-documents', dating from the period itself: in other words diaries rather than memoirs. Where we have made use of memoirs or novels, in a number of cases written long after the event, we have generally chosen authors who added something special by the clarity of their observations or the particular manner in which they put their experiences into words.

In the face of the catastrophe, the traditional difference between fiction and non-fiction did not seem as relevant as is sometimes maintained. Who can draw the line between autobiography and fiction in the novels of, for instance, Marga Minco? Who can decide whether the memoirs of Durlacher and Oberski, written after more than 30 years, are truthful or biased? The facts of the Holocaust are sufficiently known, but in order to get beyond the mere facts, fiction might be of considerable assistance. For a brief discussion of these issues, we refer to Chapter VII, the Epilogue, where we deal with the implications of representing the Holocaust.

*

Chapter I gives a brief survey of the history of the Jews in Holland. From the early arrival of the Jews from Portugal and Spain in the late sixteenth century to the refugees from Germany in the Thirties of this century, Holland enjoyed a reputation of hospitality and tolerance that was rare elsewhere in Europe. Mokum Aleph, the First Town, The Jerusalem of the West, are epithets for Amsterdam which show that Jews felt at home and comfortable in that city.

Chapter II deals with the first period after the German occupation of Holland, the period when nothing seemed as bad as it would later turn out to be. Two events mark the beginning and the end of that period: the 'Aryan' declaration, required from all civil servants at the end of 1940, and the introduction of the 'Yellow Star' in May 1942. Within that period, life for the Jews went from being bearable to bad and finally to being unlivable. In the end the choice was between being deported or going into hiding, a choice that was not as easy as it might seem in retrospect.

In Chapter III it is argued that this choice only existed for relatively few people. Holland is a small country with no mountains, no forests, no vast empty stretches of land. The conditions for a successful life outside regular society, let alone armed resistance, are more difficult than elsewhere. Going into hiding was therefore not a viable possibility for the large majority of Jews. In the remainder of the chapter, the way the deportations were organised is discussed. How did people react when they were rounded up and sent to the transit camps of Westerbork and – in a minority of cases – Vught?

Life in the transit camps Westerbork and Vught is described in Chapter IV. On the surface it almost seemed possible to lead some semblance of a normal existence there, but it soon became clear that a sharp division ran through the camp: before and after Tuesday morning. That was the time the weekly train left from Westerbork for what were called 'labour camps in the East'. The scramble to stay out of that train, the plotting, the desperate schemes – it makes for depressing reading.

In Chapter V proceedings in the actual extermination camps are discussed: we refer in particular to Auschwitz-Birkenau and Sobibor, because the majority of Dutch Jews were sent to those camps. However, the practices in camps like Majdanek, Belzec and Treblinka did not differ considerably. We also discuss Bergen-Belsen and Theresienstadt as two other important destinations for Dutch Jews. We rely heavily on the accounts of survivors, because no amount of factual description can do justice to what took place there.

Chapter VI should have been of a rather happier nature: the survivors returning to Holland. It is not. What awaited the returning Jews in Holland was probably all the more disappointing because the hope of seeing one's relatives and neighbours again had kept many going. They found that not only most of their relatives had been killed, but in too many instances their neighbours behaved as if they had never known them. A particularly low point was the lack of understanding on the part of the authorities in the struggle over Jewish war orphans, culminating in the actual kidnapping of at least two Jewish girls and hiding them in a convent abroad.

In Chapter VII – the Epilogue – we discuss briefly the theoretical background of the Holocaust debate; where has it taken us in these 50 years? It is often said that the Holocaust is indescribable, that the experience of the Shoah is beyond words and beyond reason. The many books written about it testify to the opposite. They may have been difficult to write, they are certainly not easy to read, but in a great many cases they succeed in what they want to achieve: the voice of the individual that suffered and died in the extermination camps of the Third Reich has not been lost.

*

A few remarks about the terminology: in general, we have used the term 'Holocaust' for the extermination of European Jewry, simply because it is the term that is most widely known. Sometimes, we use 'Shoah' for variation, but it is completely synonymous with Holocaust. Other terms one sometimes sees, like Ch'urban or Judeocide, we do not use at all, either because they are too unfamiliar – as is the case with the former – or because they are too specific, as is the case with Judeocide. We are aware that the National-Socialist program of 'racial purity' involved other groups, who were also deemed inferior, as well: homosexuals, gypsies, the physically and mentally handicapped, Jehovah's Witnesses, pacifists, communists. The word 'Holocaust' comprises that whole edifice of 'racial hygiene', even though in the Dutch context more than 95% of all Holocaust victims were Jews.

We conclude each chapter with a short biographical note about the experiences of Anne Frank and her family. Anne Frank has become one of the most familiar faces of the Holocaust: many people have read her diary or seen the play or one of the films made about her. The Anne Frank Foundation in Amsterdam has put a travelling exhibition together that has visited more than 50 countries and has been seen by millions. It is no exaggeration to say that her face with the sad shy smile is one of the icons of this century, a present-day Mona Lisa.

This is not the place to wonder about the reasons for her lasting popularity, nor will we try to answer the question of why she has been given this seminal role. Certainly not because she typically represents the more than one-and-a-half million Jewish children who were murdered in the Holocaust. She does not, nor can she, represent the suffering of so many other children in the ghettos of Warsaw or Lodz, or the children who died at the hands of the *Einsatzgruppen* or the police battalions. It is true that in the end her fate was the same as that of millions of others, but that was long after the diary had stopped. Most readers, therefore, will not visualise her sad end in one of the piles of corpses of Bergen-Belsen. One can sympathise with S. Dresden when he assumes that the reason for the popularity of her diary is that it is not 'terrible enough'. The reader, he argues, can only identify with small doses of suffering.

We felt, on the other hand, that amidst the bewildering array of facts and events it would be helpful to follow a thread, to see how the decrees and orders of the German authorities interfered with one individual life. Sources about the life of Anne Frank, apart from her own diary, are many and varied. A brief discussion of the most recent of these sources follows after Chapter VI.

I
Dutch Jewry before 10 May 1940

In what other country can one enjoy such complete freedom, where else can one go to sleep without fear? (Descartes)

No German should be asked to live under the same roof with Jews...We must expel them from our houses and living areas. (Das Schwarze Korps, 24 November 1938)

The Netherlands is situated at the mouth of one of Europe's most important waterways, the river Rhine. This means it holds a very strategic position, from an economic as well as from a cultural point of view. The Republic of the Seven United Provinces – as The Netherlands (i.e. Low Countries) was called before they became a unitary state under the House of Orange in 1815[1] – owed its wealth mainly to this favourable geographical position. The country was in the middle of the economically and culturally most powerful countries of Western Europe: Great Britain, France and the several German states.

Due to this strategic position, trade was as inevitable as it was profitable. In the seventeenth century the Republic was the richest nation of Europe. Dutch merchantmen voyaged to all corners of the earth. Amsterdam was not only the staple market for grain, but also for tropical products. At the local stock exchange shares of the Dutch East India Company (V.O.C.) and Dutch West India Company (W.I.C.) were bought and sold.

The 'Golden Age' was primarily due to the Republic's flourishing trade with its rich colonies, controlled by powerful companies. The greatest of these was the V.O.C., which exercised sovereign rights throughout the whole of the Indonesian archipelago. Its main source of income was the profitable trade in spices with the vast island-empire in the East, the present Indonesia. The most important slave trader between Africa and the American continent, the W.I.C. concentrated its efforts on the Americas, where the Dutch founded New Amsterdam. It was renamed New York in 1667 after it was exchanged with the English for Dutch Guyana, now Surinam. Until long into the eighteenth century, the Republic would be the most powerful colonial nation, while Amsterdam remained the financial centre of Europe with the oldest stock exchange of the world.

To use this favourable position optimally, it was essential for the Dutch elite to speak English, German and French. This was necessary, if only to prevent a small country like Holland being reduced to nothing more than a satellite. The Dutch have performed this balancing act between their mighty neighbours successfully for many centuries.

An important condition for the success of this small Republic – a federation of semi-autonomous provinces born during the sixteenth century in the long struggle for independence from Spain, the so-called Eighty Years War – was its ability to leave all their own identity and to incorporate foreign cultures within its own society without too many problems. The Republic was the first pluriform society of Europe, as was evident from the opportunities available for women and Jews. Although there seems to have been little opposition against slavery, at the University of Leiden a black man, Jacobus Capitein, was educated to become a Protestant minister, the only one in Western Europe. A climate of blissful unity in disparity prevailed. Many refugees found a safe haven in the republic against political and religious persecutions in their own countries. There were thorough theological debates, but that fact in itself is proof that in general people could say and write what they felt. It was for this reason that the French philosopher René Descartes came to Holland in the seventeenth century: *In what other country can one enjoy such complete freedom, where else can one go to sleep without fear?* he asked.

It explains why the republic became an important centre for science and philosophy. Although historians these days agree that the tolerance of the Republic was closely connected with the burgeoning economic climate, the famous cultural-historian Johan Huizinga (1872-1945), hardly a mystic, considered the cultural history of Holland in the seventeenth century an inexplicable miracle.

It stands to reason that such a place would attract refugees. The first time a considerable number of Jews came to the Republic was at the end of the sixteenth century and the beginning of the seventeenth century. These first Jews came from Portugal and Spain, where they were being forced by the Spanish Inquisition to convert to Catholicism. They settled as Catholic merchants in the rapidly growing economy of Holland. They and other immigrants were primarily welcomed because of the important contribution they made to the wealth of the country. Many of these Jews would later reconvert to Judaism, which they could practise openly.

Holland was the most important province of the Republic of the Seven United Netherlands. The Republic had just risen against the King of Spain, who tried to suppress the rebellion of Dutch noblemen and to stamp out protestantism. Fleeing the persecution of the Inquisition, these Sephardim (Sefarad is Hebrew for Spain) contributed in no small measure to the growth of overseas commerce, in particular the trade in sugar and slaves, the tobacco, silk and diamond industry, and finance.[2] Some of these Sephardic Jews managed to become very wealthy. They were involved in many cultural and social activities and would become the inspiration for many of Rembrandt's paintings; the philosopher Baruch de Spinoza came from this milieu.

Subsequent Jewish immigrants did not fare so well: the German Jews or Ashkenazim (Ashkenas means Germany) came from the east of Europe at the beginning of the seventeenth century. Driven out of Poland and the eastern parts of Germany by bloody pogroms, they differed from their Spanish co-religionists in language, in traditions and customs, even in the clothes they wore. They had no part in the culture or in the wealth of the Sephardim. From the late 1630s two different congregations (Sephardim and Ashkenazim) existed within the Jewish community. The Sephardim were by far the smaller group. It is estimated that in 1672, of a total population of 180,000, there were approximately 2500 Sephardim and 5000 Ashkenazim in Amsterdam, with (much) smaller numbers in the other cities of the Republic.

A certain animosity between both groups would be a constant factor in the history of the Jews in Holland. Only in the course of the nineteenth century did the Ashkenazic and Sephardic communities become success-fully integrated into Dutch society.

Both groups found a place of refuge in Holland in a period when Europe was embroiled in religious wars. It was, for instance, impossible for Jews to settle in England or France. In Holland they did not have to wear prescribed signs on their clothing, nor did they have to live in ghettos, as in Venice. They were free to practise their religion, alongside the Calvinist majority and minorities of Lutherans, Catholics, Remonstrants and Men-nonites. The only thing they were not allowed to do was to try and convert Christians or challenge Christian theology. The reverse obviously was not prohibited. Yet they enjoyed a freedom of speech and thought unknown elsewhere in Europe. Jews were not only tolerated, but could actually publish their own sacred and learned texts and even open seminaries.

In a description of the city of Amsterdam from 1662, M. Fokkens writes about the new Portuguese synagogue and obviously wants to inform his fellow citizens of Amsterdam about the interesting habits of this strange new 'sect':

The Portuguese hold a fairly large place, that has been built upon the site of two houses; downstairs there is a large empty courtyard with a water-barrel, which is opened with a tap; on top there is a towel, because Jews first wash their hands before they enter their Church; there are stairs on both sides; then one enters their Church; the women are on the top gallery, separated from the men. They cannot see each other; at the end of the Church there is a large wooden cupboard, that is opened with two doors: in it many precious things, among others the books of Moses, clothed in beautifully crocheted draperies; their Teachers stand a little higher – about three feet higher – than the rest of the congregation; the men wear a white scarf over their hat, which covers shoulders and body. They all hold a little booklet in their hand, written in Hebrew. Their Sabbath begins on Friday evening, when the sun goes down; then they all light the lamps in their homes as well as in their Church; they burn until Saturday evening, when their Sabbath is over, because the Jews count the beginning of the days from one evening to the next; in their Churches they burn a light in their Glass Lamp continuously; during some religious holidays they light the crowns and big

silver chandeliers in their Churches, which are worth a lot; during Sabbath they
dress beautifully and don't do any work. (Gans, 1971:46, own translation)

As the Dutch cultural-historian Johan Huizinga has commented, this remarkable freedom of religion had less to do with principles of tolerance
than with the kind of pragmatism and common sense that, par excellence,
characterised this merchant state. One of the reasons behind this attitude
of laissez-faire was that it was a great deal cheaper to have a tolerant
government in a divided nation – more than 35% of which was Catholic –
than to exercise cruel repression.

The authorities left the Jews in peace as long as they adhered to three
important conditions:

1 It was forbidden to libel Christendom in word or in writing;

2 It was forbidden to try and convert a Christian to become a Jew;

3 It was forbidden to have sexual relations with Christian women (even
prostitutes).

In Dutch society the Jews would never be more than a small minority; their
total would never amount to more than 2% of the entire population. Most
of them lived in Amsterdam, where at the end of the eighteenth century
they constituted nearly 12% of the population. In the rest of the Republic,
many towns and rural areas did not allow Jews before 1795, or only in
limited numbers. Everywhere they were subjected to a number of constrict-
ing measures, in particular excluding them from membership of the most
important guilds[3] and from a number of other professions, including
shopkeeping. This did not prevent some of them from growing very rich,
usually from banking. William III of Orange, in 1688 about to become King
of England, managed to finance his enterprise only by borrowing huge
sums of money from the Jewish bankers of Suasso. And a French visitor to
the Low Countries wrote in 1736 after a visit to the Tulpenburg estate of
David de Pinto just outside of Amsterdam:

A une lieue d'Amsterdam nous descendimes chez le juif Pinto, riche et très
honnête homme à la religion près. Il a le plus beau jardin de toute la Hollande.
(*'We went to the place of the Jew Pinto near Amsterdam, a rich and very decent man,
except for matters of religion. He has the most beautiful garden in the whole of Holland'*)
(Gans, 1971:114, own translation)

In 1795 French revolutionary armies occupied The Netherlands. The old
order collapsed, the *Batavian Republic* was established, and soon thereafter,
in 1796, civil equality of the Jews became law: from now on they were
granted full civil rights on equal footing with every other Dutch subject.
The restrictive settlement laws directed against the Jews were abolished.

They obtained their place as citizens in a country that many had considered their own for a long time. By this time their number had grown to around 30,000.

The end of French rule and the inauguration of a constitutional monarchy under the House of Orange in 1815 did not reverse the judicial and political emancipation of the Jews. This emancipation would be completed in 1919 with the introduction of universal suffrage for men and women. Only then did the large majority of poor Jews benefit fully from the formal emancipation of 1796. Political emancipation was to be the first step to the social and cultural emancipation of Dutch Jewry, which took shape in the course of the nineteenth century. The government stimulated the learning of Dutch as a means of social integration. Yiddish gradually disappeared, and the use of Yiddish expressions became confined to household customs.

During the 18th century a serious economic recession had taken hold in Holland – culminating in the virtual bankruptcy of the Dutch East India Company (V.O.C.) in 1796 – and it was not until the second half of the nineteenth century that a slow process of industrialization and modernization was started. The Jews not only profited from the dynamics of this economic, cultural and scientific upswing after 1870, but also contributed considerably to its development.

Until then, the great majority of Dutch Jewry had lived in poverty as hawkers and small-time traders. After the French occupation of the country and the subsequent lifting of the restrictive settlement laws, they had gained access to other professions, but the number of Jews in 'typically Jewish' occupations like trading remained considerable. Only with industrialization and mechanization at the end of the nineteenth century did their numbers increase in other professions like printing, diamond-cutting, textile, metal and food industries. In particular, the diamond industry in Amsterdam profited from the discovery of large quantities of rough diamonds in South Africa and a strongly increased demand for cut diamonds in America.

At the same time, Jews began to play an increasingly important role in public life, in political movements such as the liberal and, especially, the socialist parties. They took a great interest in issues like universal suffrage, the emancipation of women, the institution of public utilities and the curbing of the complete freedom of enterprise through social legislation. Characteristic of many Jews was their strongly developed sense of social justice. This explains their contributions to the early labour movement and to socialism. The union of diamond workers, for instance, was one of the first and most influential unions founded at the end of the nineteenth century. It is difficult to overestimate the importance of these unions for the Jewish proletariat; they contributed among others to the process of secularization.

In general, the Jewish proletariat was more in favour of socialism than of Zionism. Furthermore, these unions made an important contribution to the cultural uplifting of the Jewish working class. Jews were also overrepresented in cultural and intellectual life, in the sciences and in music. Before the Second World War more than 20% of artists in the lively world of entertainment in Amsterdam were Jews.

*

Nineteenth-century emancipation had caused a variety of reactions, one of which was antisemitism. Many enlightened Jews and non-Jews considered assimilation as the only remedy against this. Because only mild forms of antisemitism and anti-Judaism had ever occurred in Holland, relatively few Jews had seriously considered conversion to Christianity. Elsewhere in Europe, baptism was considered the traditional *ticket to European culture*, as German poet Heinrich Heine had called it. Besides, Jews underwent a process of secularization. They felt a growing reluctance to identify themselves with Jewish religion, and Jewish children usually went to the normal public schools. Mixed marriages were another way to integrate into Dutch society, although the argument for integration became less and less important as secularization increased. The price paid for this remarkably successful emancipation was a partial loss of the traditional knowledge of Jewish religion and culture. Many Jews became unfamiliar with the *Bible*, that is, the Old Testament. Circumcision, religious marriages and funerals might be kept up, but the observance of the sabbath and dietary laws rapidly declined. Jewish culture became limited to starched tablecloths, chicken soup and gefilte fish on sabbath evening, but for the rest it became quaint and obsolete. The large majority were nominally members of an orthodox congregation and went to the synagogue on religious holidays, but religious laws were no concern of theirs. The humanist system of education had caused a deep-rooted secularization; the result was that before the war, only a small minority of Jews considered themselves truly observant.

Jews were no longer different in appearance from other Dutchmen: traditional dress, beard and sideburns had disappeared. The value that traditionally had been attached to study and intellectual pursuits in the days of the diaspora had now been translated into participation and integration into Dutch society.

However, this should not imply that they did not feel Jewish, no matter how indifferent their Jewishness appeared. For most of them Jewish heritage and Jewish traditions remained important. Even most of the socialists among them kept up their ties with Judaism. The Jews remained a recognizable group, if only by the maintenance of a separate subcultural tradition as a minority. The process that had been started in the nineteenth century among the Jews of Holland may therefore perhaps be better characterised as acculturation, rather than as structural assimilation.

Before the Second World War the large majority of the Jews lived in the three main cities: Amsterdam, Rotterdam and The Hague. More than 60% lived in Amsterdam: it was the centre of Jewish Holland with – at least on

Sunday market in Jewish Amsterdam

the surface – a picturesque neighbourhood, the soul of Jewish Amsterdam. In reality, the Jewish proletariat of Amsterdam was seriously impoverished. Unsanitary housing conditions and considerable social problems existed everywhere, but especially in the old densely populated 'Jodenbuurt', the Jewish Quarter, around the two synagogues.

*

What was Dutch society like just before the Second World War? In most European countries the First World War had meant the beginning of what Paul Fussell once called 'modern memory', a memory which could neither fathom the experienced horrors of the war nor cope with it in terms of the traditional values of Fatherland, Glory and Honor. The Great War had led philosophers, authors, poets and artists to express the idea that something irreparable had occurred and that even Western civilization was mortal. They realised that education, science and technology could also be used for destructive purposes. Knowledge and the existing morals had become suspect. In 1922, the English poet T.S. Eliot put the feeling of utter despondency among intellectuals into words with his poem, *The Waste Land*. Modern movements like surrealism and dadaism went even further in their mockery of everything that had been holy in that rotten lost civilisation: God, patriotism, monogamous marriage.

Holland, however, had remained neutral during the First World War. The result of this neutrality was that the rude disturbance of nineteenth-century illusions had not taken place[4] – the doctrine of bourgeois morality had not been shaken. As late as 1900, going to a concert, even a performance of the Passion of St. Matthew by J.S. Bach, was seen as something 'worldly' by many Protestants. The increasing popularity after 1920 of radio and especially film was met with stubborn resistance by the church authorities. Film and jazz were looked upon as signs of the 'americanization' of cultural life. The same promotion of vulgarity and immorality was perceived in other art forms. Showing female nudity was far from accepted in Dutch museums, and compared with lively cultural centres like Berlin, Paris, Vienna and London, most Dutch cities seemed like boarding schools for upper class girls. Before the Second World War there were restrictions on mixed swimming, a strict Board of Film Censors tried to uphold morality, and in some cities it was forbidden to dance. Christian values were defended by the very conservative churches of Holland, which had a great deal of influence. Because of the large gap between Catholics and Protestants, between believers and non-believers, Holland's was a culture of sub-cultures, divided into separate communities: the Protestant and the Catholic, whereas the non-believers were divided between the 'capitalist' bourgeoisie and the 'red' working class. Dutch society of the Thirties is therefore sometimes called a 'pillarised' or 'compartmentalised' society. There were Protestant and Catholic women's organisations, youth movements, radio stations, newspapers, soccer leagues, societies for chicken farming, and so on. The German author Konrad Merz (ps. of Kurt Lehmann), who fled to Holland after Hitler's take-over in 1933, was so amazed by this phenomenon that he wrote in his book, *Ein Mensch fällt aus Deutschland* (A Man Falls From Germany):

> They have here a Catholic cattle-breeders union and a Protestant one, a Protestant hairdresser and a Catholic one, a Catholic trader in colonial spices and a Protestant trader in colonial spices, and it never happens that a Catholic has his hair cut by a Protestant, or the other way around. One feels, coming from Germany, this country has not been through the war. And often it seems to me that a flight to Holland is like a flight into past decades. (Merz, 1981:90, own translation)

Even though the Jews adapted in their willingness to integrate with this segmented society and its many unwritten laws, they did not develop a tight organizational network to buttress their particular belief systems and interests as did the other Dutch religious groupings. But in another sense they adapted well to the Dutch mentality as far as they adopted an overtly trusting attitude towards public authority.

Mild forms of antisemitism increased from the end of the nineteenth century, but never gave rise to pogroms as in Eastern Europe. It was, for instance, not possible for a Jew to advance to a high post in the civil service;

in this, Holland was not different from other European countries. Some restaurants and dance-halls made it plain that Jews were not welcome on their premises, a form of exclusion also applicable to black Dutchmen from Surinam. Abel Herzberg, Jacques Presser and Louis de Jong, the outstanding historians of the Holocaust in Holland, all report having experienced mild forms of antisemitism in their youth. In *Bitter Herbs*, Marga Minco writes about these early forms of antisemitism; they can only be characterised as insignificant when compared with the far greater evil that was to follow:

> I frequently asked myself why we were different. 'Our teacher says Jews are bad people,' a neighbour's child once said to me. He went to a Catholic school. 'You murdered Jesus.' At that time I didn't yet know who Jesus was (...) When we grew older, we hardly noticed any of this any more. Children below the age of ten are often crueller than grown-ups. I do remember that we had a Catholic housemaid who had to ask the priest's permission before coming to work for us. The priest approved; he even told her she did not have to eat fish on Friday. That was a stroke of luck for her, for on the evening before the Sabbath we ate a very elaborate dinner, and all sorts of meat dishes were served at table. (Minco, 1960:8/9)

Aggressive manifestations of antisemitism invariably provoked public indignation; it was considered 'unchic' and 'not respectable.'

Even the Dutch fascist party, the National Socialist Movement or NSB – founded in 1931 – adopted antisemitism only at the end of the Thirties, influenced by Nazism in neighbouring Germany. This radicalization did not make the Movement more popular: during the last election before the German occupation, the party polled only 4% of the votes. By adopting antisemitism the party had alienated itself even more from the bulk of the Dutch electorate.

*

The Jewish issue did become a problem when large groups of Jewish refugees began to come to Holland in search of a safe haven. From the end of the nineteenth century – particularly after the pogroms in Poland and Russia in the Eighties and Nineties – Jews had fled to Holland, and after 1933 they were joined by refugees from Germany. Between 1933 and 1939 about 30,000 (of an estimated 500,000) German Jews would eventually cross the Dutch border. Among them were the families Frank and Durlacher. Gerard Durlacher, born in 1928 in Baden-Baden, Germany, clearly remembers 30 January 1933, the day Hitler came to power:

> My mother puts her finger to her lips. All of a sudden the voices on the air fall silent, too. Forks and knives freeze in mid air. A hoarse, excited voice reports from Berlin that the new Chancellor of the German Reich is ... Adolf Hitler. Adolf,

Seider in Amsterdam in the 1930's

just like my uncle (...) Kneeling on a chair, wrapped in Grandmother's shawl, I look outside and see something that makes me speechless. On both sides of the street, as far as the eye can see, there are long rows of torchlights, like curling snakes of fire. The cold, damp air quivers like turbulent water. Under their helmets, the faces of the Brownshirts reflect the flames. Hundreds of devils stamp their hooves on the granite paving stones and roar their song. Flags flutter above the flames and cast black shadows on the houses. Men of iron wearing helmets of steel pound their boots on the anvil of the street. (Durlacher, 1993:21/22)

Jewish Relief Committees were formed to make life as bearable as possible for these refugees. There was, for instance, a competent welfare organization used to dealing with young refugees, including those who took their chance outrunning the border guards. The relief organizations were not merely a means of fulfilling a charitable obligation, but represented an important statement about their own role within Dutch society.

There was, however, a certain animosity among the Jews themselves. Eastern European Jewish refugees had been in Holland since the 1880s. They were poor, but because of their industriousness they had been accepted by the older Jewish population of Amsterdam. However, the often well-to-do German Jewish refugees of the Thirties did not always fit in. In a sense some of them had become so assimilated that they seemed to behave in a more German manner than the 'Aryan' Germans themselves, and felt the need to tell everybody how much better everything had been *bei uns in Deutschland* – before Hitler, of course.

During the first years of the Hitler regime, only a handful of people in Holland recognised the essentially criminal character of the new regime. Primarily, it was the German Jewish refugees – together with political refugees like communists and social-democrats – and a few Dutch intellectuals, like the author Menno ter Braak[5], who sounded the alarm bell against the dangers of Nazism. Protests against the persecution of the Jews were limited to these intellectuals and a small group of politically active Zionists. Some Jews looked upon Zionism as the answer to the increasing violence against Jews in Europe. But most Jews in Holland felt they were first and foremost Dutch citizens, even those who had arrived relatively recently.

One such was Milo Anstadt, a Polish Jew, who fled to Holland with his family:

> Politically, I felt cosmopolitan and absolutely not Jewish-oriented. I had no affinity with Jewish religion. I rejected Zionism, because I couldn't see how it could provide a solution for seventeen million Jews living all over the world... I felt strongly inclined to assimilate and was not interested in my Jewishness. I was not a Jew out of my own free will, but because the world had labelled me so. (Anstadt, 1995:235, own translation).

It became clear after Hitler's take-over in Germany that antisemitism was to be the essence of his ideology. It started with the boycott of Jewish businesses and the burning of books written by Jewish and Marxist authors in 1933. Gerard Durlacher remembers the day his grandmother's furniture store attracted an unusual crowd:

> Huge men in the brown uniform of the Stormtroopers are positioned on either side of the doorway with their revolvers strapped to their Sam Browne belts and their legs encased in shiny black boots. They are standing as still as statues. Beside them, mounted on poles, are large placards with words I can understand even though I can't read. Rowdy boys, heads taller than I am, shout the slogans, while the adults, in their musty worn-out clothes mutter their approval or nod their heads in agreement. 'Don't buy from Jews, they will be your downfall' and 'Jews are ruining the nation. Germans, put a stop to this now!' Stars of David have been scrawled on the broad store windows with whitewash, dripping towards the corners in long white streaks and ruining the beautiful new black marble frame. (Durlacher, 1993:33/34)

Well-known opponents of the regime fled from Germany. The large majority of Jews in the Reich believed (or rather hoped) things would be all right, notwithstanding the almost constant antisemitic hate propaganda in the press. They felt so German anyway that it was difficult to perceive that they were no longer welcome in their own country. After all, they shared a history going back a thousand years. Many had fought bravely in the First

World War. German industry, science and culture relied heavily on Jewish talent. This, however, proved no guarantee. In 1935 the so-called Nuremberg Laws were passed: citizenship in the Reich was from now on limited to those of *German or kindred blood*. Marriages and sexual intercourse between Jews and Aryans were forbidden. Durlacher gives an impression of what it was like to be a Jewish boy in a school where the rest of the class, former friends, suddenly became hostile, because he did not belong to the 'superior' race:

> At least ten of our classmates are standing on the school steps around Fritz in the brown uniform of the 'Young Folk'. Their belt buckles are gleaming and their brown shirts have been freshly ironed, as if their club is having a party. They radiate belligerence, and the older boys, similarly outfitted in brown, treat them with more camaraderie than usual (...) Slowly but surely, the brown and red pack catches up with us. They are strangers, our classmates. Hungry wolves in the snow. (Durlacher, 1993:72)

In 1938 it became clear to even the most optimistic Jews that there was no future for them in Germany. In that year, more organised and officially sanctioned violence began, first in annexed Austria in the spring of that year and then over the whole of Germany, culminating in the November 'Kristallnacht' pogrom, cynically named after the broken glass and windows of Jewish shops and houses. On that night of 9/10 November 1938, synagogues were burnt down all over Germany, Jewish shops looted and burnt, dozens of innocent citizens murdered and many thousands injured, arrested and taken to concentration camps. To accommodate so many new prisoners, the concentration camps of Buchenwald, Dachau and Sachsenhausen were expanded.

Forty years later, on a journey back to the days and places of his childhood, Gerard Durlacher sought out the place of the synagogue in Baden-Baden:

> The white stone synagogue, with its slender pillars, arched windows, multi-colored rosettes and broad staircase whose steps I had trouble climbing as a child, no longer exists. It has been replaced by a garage housing a few trucks. Not a trace remains of the place where, on the evening of 9 November 1938, black-uniformed SS men forced elderly Jews to uncover their heads and sing Nazi songs, with their faces turned towards the Ark containing the holy Torah scrolls, which flicker like the burning bush after having been set ablaze under the roars and jeers of the Death's Head Regiment. (Durlacher, 1993: 96/97)

The direct consequence of Kristallnacht was a confused scramble to get out of Germany: an endless stream of refugees trying to reach the Dutch, Belgian and Swiss borderposts. Because of the continuing economic crisis and high unemployment – the impact of the financial crash of 1929 in Wall Street seems to have lingered longer in Holland than in most other countries

One of the Jewish children from Eastern Europe,
passing through Holland on one of the children's transports

– the Dutch government was not prepared to shelter and house large groups of Jewish immigrants. The government also felt it had to keep pace with immigration restrictions elsewhere in Western Europe. The authorities tried to dam the stream as much as possible, and many were sent back as *unwanted aliens* at the border. Illegal immigrants were interned in special camps. In 1939 the Dutch government had a large camp built – at the expense of Dutch Jewry – in a relatively sparsely populated area in the northeast of Holland, camp Westerbork.

All in all, in the five years between 1933 and 1938, some 130,000 of the roughly 500,000 German Jews left their homeland – usually leaving their property, possessions and wealth behind. After Kristallnacht another 118,000 escaped – now going to any country that would take them. Even after the war had started, a further 30,000 still managed to leave the Reich. About half of the original Jewish population remained in Germany.

In Dutch Jewish circles the fear grew that the settlement of large groups of 'foreign' Jews in Holland would lead to increased antisemitism. Therefore, the relief committees directed their support towards stimulating further emigration (to England and the USA). Many owe their lives to the initiatives and endeavours of a few, like Mrs Truus Wijsmuller, who organised 74 childrens' transports from Austria and Germany to England. Almost 10,000 children found temporary shelter in Holland, Belgium and Great Britain, before most of them were taken to the USA or Palestine.

Meanwhile, many books and pamphlets describing the persecutions in Germany had appeared, and numerous stories about the ruthless treatment of Jews circulated, many of them told by the victims themselves. *Ein Mensch fällt aus Deutschland* (1936) by Konrad Merz gives a stark impression of life in exile. The Dutch critic Menno ter Braak praised it as the *first real emigré-novel*.

Amsterdam became the centre of an 'emigrant' literature, although most authors were only travelling through to settle elsewhere. Amsterdam also gained from the flood of German, mainly Jewish, artistes. One of the first was the anti-Fascist Ernst Busch, who performed leftwing songs in the *Kabaret der Katakomben* (Cabaret of the Catacombs), accompanied on the piano by composer Hans Eisler. In Holland Ernst Busch had gained a reputation as a singer in the *Dreigroschen Oper* (Threepenny Opera) by Bertolt Brecht and Kurt Weill. These artistes introduced a new kind of cabaret from Berlin: the cabaret-revue. Amsterdam, with Bern and Zürich, became the cradle of the 'emigré-cabarets'. Willy Rosen, who was not allowed to perform in Germany after 1933, founded the *Theater der Prominenten* in Amsterdam in 1937, a cabaret company of escaped Jewish artistes. The company was constantly supplied with new performers. Many were famous German artistes waiting for visas to America. Some never received the necessary documents. *Die Pfeffermühle* (The Peppermill) became a famous satirical cabaret under the leadership of Erika Mann, the daughter of author Thomas Mann and wife of English poet W.H. Auden. But the ridiculing of Adolf Hitler, a 'friendly Head of State', was not appreciated by the Dutch authorities, no matter how culturally valid: foreigners had to abstain from political activities. *Die Pfeffermühle* was not the only group of German emigrés to experience this.

As early as April 1933, *unwanted aliens* were sometimes handed back to German border officials. This nearly always meant concentration camp or prison. In 1934, for instance, the German government exerted pressure on the Dutch government to put the communist Jewish author and refugee Heinz Liepmann on trial, because in his novel *Das Vaterland* (The Fatherland) he had criticised Hitler. He was sentenced to one month in prison, in Holland. German pressure proved effective in a number of other cases as well. Even before the occupation of Holland, Dutch and German police found it easy to work together.

*

The noose around the neck of the Jews in Germany was being tightened all the time. The multitude of coercive measures enacted by the state – almost two thousand laws and administrative regulations – had made them into a caste of pariahs. After the discrimination, the isolation and the elimination from economic, cultural and public life, all they still seemed permitted to do was to breathe.

On 30 January 1939 Hitler announced in the Reichstag *the destruction of the Jewish race in Europe in the coming war*. After the German surprise attack on Poland in September 1939, the English and French governments declared war on Hitler. The Second World War had begun.

Anne Frank

Among the many thousands of Jews who settled in Amsterdam between 1933 and 1939 were the Franks from Frankfurt am Main, a bustling industrial city and financial centre. The forefathers of Otto Frank had lived in that city for centuries, achieving a modest position of wealth and prestige in the world of commerce and banking. Otto, born in 1889, the same year as Adolf Hitler, seemed destined to follow in his father's and grandfather's footsteps and become a banker. When he was 20, he spent some time in America, studying and working and preparing himself for his professional career. He was a cultured man with many interests: he liked music and German literature, among other things. After the First World War he would develop a passion for photography – he owned one of the first commercially available Leica cameras. Not too long after his return from the USA, the First World War broke out. Otto Frank had no hesitation in serving his country as best he could. He loved Germany. The fact that he came from a Jewish family background made no difference to him. The family had assimilated long ago, Jewish orthodoxy meant very little to him. His first allegiance was no doubt to the German 'fatherland'. At the front he was quickly promoted to 2nd lieutenant. One incident from that war is typical of the man. When the end of hostilities was announced on 11 November 1918, his family in Frankfurt were relieved that, to their knowledge, Otto had survived unharmed. But they had to wait a long time before he came home. Only in January 1919 did he show up in his native town. Then he told his worried mother that at the end of the war he had had to requisition a couple of horses from a Belgian farmer, leaving the man desperate. Otto had promised him that, if he could, he would bring the man's horses back personally. So that is what he had done: he had given his word, and a German officer does not go back on that.

After the war Otto Frank decided not to go into banking, but to follow an industrial career instead. In 1925 he married Edith Holländer, from Aachen. One year later their first daughter, Margot, was born and in 1929, on 12 June, their second, Annelise Marie.

The second half of the Twenties had been a time of increasing prosperity in Germany: the effects of the war and subsequent defeat seemed to have been overcome, and people were looking towards the future with confidence. The crash of the stock exchange in New York changed all that. Confidence and optimism rapidly turned into gloom and despair, when first thousands, and then millions lost their jobs. This paved the way for extremist parties, one of which was led by Adolf Hitler. He promised **Arbeit und Brot** (Work and Bread); the German workers were prepared to go a long way in order to get it. Once in power, Hitler set about to fully implement his program: Jews and Germans had to be separated from each other.

Otto Frank could not have foreseen all the implications of Hitler's anti-Jewish measures, but he sensed no good could come from the new government when – in the summer of 1933 – the city of Frankfurt decided that from then on Jewish children had to go to separate schools. When the opportunity arose to leave Frankfurt and to set up a Dutch branch of his chemical firm, Opekta, he did not hesitate long. He went to Amsterdam, and once he had settled there he wrote to his wife suggesting she should join him in the New Year. So Edith came with the oldest of the two girls, Margot, and Anne followed at the beginning of 1934. Otto had found comfortable accommodation on the second floor of a new housing estate in the south of Amsterdam, Merwedeplein 37. There Anne and Margot grew up like two ordinary Dutch schoolgirls, soon speaking Dutch fluently. Anne attended the VIth Amsterdam Montessori school in the Niersstraat, close to her home. The Merwedeplein and surrounding streets became a centre of activities for Jewish refugees from Germany: that was nice for Anne and Margot, even nicer for Edith, who never learned to speak Dutch properly. Anne's two best friends were also daughters of refugees, Hannah Goslar and (Su)Sanne Ledermann. Only Hannah Goslar survived the war.

Anne was a quick learner at school, popular with teachers and other children alike, albeit that the former did sometimes become exasperated with her excessive talking. Hannah Goslar remembers how her mother used to say: 'God knows everything, but Anne Frank knows everything better.'

Summing up the period between 1933 to 1940, one may say that the Frank girls had adapted well to their Dutch environment and that the future looked promising for both of them. All that would soon change.

II
From Aryan Declaration to Yellow Star

The Antechamber of Death

I feel certain that further troubles will not bring any Jew back to the paths of righteousness; on the contrary, I think that upon experiencing such great anguish they will think that there is no God at all in the universe, because had there been a God He would not have let such things happen to His people. (Moshe Flinker, November 26, 1942)

...it was in the first instance the Jewish race which only received my prophecies with laughter when I said that (...) I would then among other things settle the Jewish problem. Their laughter was uproarious, but I think that for some time now they have been laughing on the other side of their face. (Hitler, speech of January 30, 1939)

After a blitzkrieg of just five days, which began in the early hours of 10 May 1940, German troops occupied Holland. The country had long maintained a policy of strict neutrality and was neither mentally nor materially prepared for war. The bombardment of Rotterdam, which killed nearly 1000 people, and the German warning that more cities would follow, was sufficient reason for the Dutch Government to capitulate. Queen Wilhelmina and her government went into exile in London to continue the struggle from there and to protect their colonial interests in the Dutch East and West Indies. Their departure created a moral vacuum which was to cause a great deal of confusion among Dutch civil servants. An illustration of this can be found in novelist W.F. Hermans' scathing attack on Dutch officialdom, *Herinneringen van een engelbewaarder* (Memories of a Guardian Angel). In this book the main character, a public prosecutor, and his circle of colleagues do their utmost to find excuses for not doing anything. They all continue as if nothing has happened, hoping a solution will present itself. They consider it their duty to prevent chaos, because:

chaos is what we have to avoid at all cost, under all circumstances. Where would we be if the whole underworld was given the chance to make a killing as well? (Hermans, 1971: 289, own translation)

Not only the Queen and her government escaped to England, thousands of others tried to do the same; among them hundreds of Jews. In 1940 a decision to leave one's home and country could not have been easy. Most people had never been away from Holland, not even on holiday. One of the few who managed to get away was the young biology student and poet Leo Vroman. In the account of his escape from Holland, called *De adem van Mars* (Mars' Breath), Vroman describes how haphazard and improvised everything was. With luck he got to Scheveningen on the coast, with luck he heard about other people planning to buy a boat to sail to England, with luck he bought himself a place on board, with luck they got out of the harbour:

> At the end of the quay there were coast guards who called out to us that the wind was good and that we had to head west. As if they had waited for this, our two sailors began to object, sailed to the shore and jumped off board: we had to fend for ourselves. One of us, whom I had originally taken for a fisherman because he wore a blue jersey, took the wheel. He said he had sailed before, and we all wanted to believe him. (Vroman, 1956:22, own translation)

The indefatigable Mrs Weismuller managed to get a number of Jewish children from Germany and Austria onto one of the last boats to England. Most of these escape attempts, however, were unsuccessful, as a consequence of blocked roads and a shortage of ships. A number of those who failed to get away in time committed suicide; sometimes even whole families ended their lives together. In *De oorlog die Hitler won* (The War That Hitler Won) H. Wielek writes how he remembers, in those May days of 1940, the couple from Vienna that he met in September 1938 in Lugano. They warned him then of the intentions of the Nazis:

> Escaped from Vienna, because the Nazis had occupied it. Fled the first day. They had seen enough. To Prague. Until the Nazis came there too. Now radically to America. On their way to the French coast with their car, which the driver is allowed to keep.

> "Please, won't you join us, within two years the whole of Europe will be dominated by the Nazis. They will not leave one Jew alone. We have seen it in Germany, Austria, Czecho-Slovakia." "Yes, ma'am, but in Holland...." "Ach, you don't know the Nazis. They have been ferreting for such a long time." "You don't know the Dutch." "You will have to decide for yourself, but one day you will think of me." (Wielek, 1947:11, own translation)[1]

On the other hand, there were Jews who took a certain pride in staying, even when they had a chance to get away. They felt they were indispensible or wished to stay out of a mistaken sense of loyalty or duty. One such person was the father of author Clarissa Jacobi, a driver with the Amsterdam municipality:

During those five days in May 1940 my father had the chance to escape to England. A cousin of his went. He could have gone with the truck of the telephone company to IJmuiden and leave the whole lot behind.

"I don't even think about it. I was mobilised for four years during 1914-1918. I am not deserting my country now. The company needs me. If you want to go, I will try to take you there, but I am staying." (Jacobi, 1977:21, own translation)

For this loyalty he would later die in Sobibor.

A dilemma of another kind was faced by families only some of whose members could get away, because there was not enough room for all. The historian Louis de Jong remembers how seven of his family tried to get into the taxi that was to take them to the coast. The driver said he could only take five. De Jong:

So two had to be left behind. Which two? We talked about this excitedly. Couldn't we take all seven. The driver stuck to his maximum. I said: "Let the old ones stay here (what were those old people going to do in England anyway?). Nobody had a better idea. Nobody had any idea at all. We became exhausted. Grandfather and grandmother accepted the verdict and went home. We got in." (De Jong, 1993:88, own translation)

In the first few months of the occupation, the new regime hid its true face. Most Dutchmen breathed a sigh of relief, thinking that it could have been so much worse. For the greater part, life went on as usual, although English and American films were soon forbidden. The Germans had installed a *Zivilverwaltung* (civil administration) to exercise supervision over the Dutch civil service, which was allowed to remain in place on condition that it served German interests.

Arthur Seyss-Inquart, an Austrian Nazi notorious for his antisemitism and his role during the 'Anschluss' between Germany and Austria in March 1938, was appointed *Reichskommissar für die besetzten Niederländischen Gebiete* (Reich Commissioner for the Occupied Dutch Territories). His initial policy was to try and win over the Dutch population for the National-Socialist cause, the 'New Order', because the Dutch were considered a Germanic brother nation. In order to gain the confidence of the population, he thought it better not to confront them with brute force, which would have been alien to the Dutch tradition of tolerance.

Therefore, he did not yet mention the ultimate aim of the Nazi government, which was to reduce the Jews in Holland to the same lowly status to which the German Jews had been reduced since 1933. Personally, he felt that Jews were enemies of the Reich *with whom we can neither come to an armistice nor to peace.*

During the course of 1940, a number of discriminatory laws were gradually introduced to achieve this purpose. To begin with all Jewish newspapers were banned in September 1940. Six months later appeared *Het Joodsche Weekblad* (The Jewish Weekly) – its content was of course controlled by the Germans. In October all Dutch civil servants had to fill in the so-called Aryan Declaration, a form about family history and possible Jewish ancestors. According to Decree 189, somebody was Jewish if he/she had *at least three Jewish grandparents*. It is characteristic of the innocence in that first year of the war as well as of the loyal conformism of the civil servants that 98% signed the Declaration. The historian Abel Herzberg remarked: *Each signed the death-warrant of his own civilisation.* For the first time in modern Dutch history, a distinctive line was drawn between Jews and non-Jews.

Once this definition existed, the occupying power could dismiss the Jews. One month later all civil servants of Jewish descent were removed from office. The Germans had shown their true colours: the Jews were on their way out.

A cold pogrom has begun, as one of the first illegal student papers put it, and a theologian prophesied in a pamphlet distributed in large numbers, which appeared under the title 'Almost too late': *They will disappear – we need not have the slightest illusion about it. They have been put out, soon they will be put down.* At the Technical University of Delft and the University of Utrecht, words of protest were heard against the removal of Jewish professors and colleagues. At the University of Leiden, Holland's oldest university founded – in 1575 – as a reward for the stubborn resistance of that city against the Spanish rulers, Professor Cleveringa, Dean of the Law Faculty, openly protested against the expulsion of Jewish colleagues. In his speech to a packed auditorium of the university, he said he did not need to elaborate on the background of those who had ordered these expulsions. *Their deed qualifies itself conclusively.* These words were followed by thunderous applause. One of the students in the auditorium remembered 20 years later what happened after Cleveringa had finished:

> There were a few moments of silence and then suddenly, without previous arrangement, we started to sing the national anthem. There were few of us who could hold back our tears. (De Jong, 1966:132, own translation)

The next day Cleveringa was arrested and kept in prison for eight months. The universities of Delft and Leiden were closed by the Germans.

*

In the course of 1941, Jews were issued with identity documents with a black letter J stamped into them. Just as the large majority of non-Jews had done concerning the Aryan Declaration, most of the Jews resigned themselves to this decree. Even they believed things could not get much worse. As we have seen, one of the characteristics of Dutch Jewry was its deferential attitude towards public authority; ironically enough, it was precisely because of their apparent integration that the Dutch Jews became such easy victims. This attitude presents a sharp contrast to the refugees of Eastern Europe who had learnt from a long history of persecutions that authorities could not always be trusted.

There are also examples of a different reaction towards the anti-Jewish policy of the Germans: L.E. Visser, the president judge of the Supreme Court of Justice, himself Jewish but not particularly religious, now went to a synagogue for the very first time in his life as an act of solidarity. He would become one of the most prominent victims: his dismissal from the Supreme Court gained a great deal of attention and drew much criticism, but passed without any of his colleagues raising their voices. This early in the occupation the soon-to-be common excuse was already being rehearsed: his colleagues decided to comply *to prevent worse*. Their staying on the Supreme Court, however, gave the impression of lending a certain legitimacy to all kinds of German measures, such as:

– *the abolition of the parliamentary system,*

– *the severe punishability of every act of resistance,*

– *the deportation of the Dutch Jews,*

– *the entering into German military service,*

– *the bringing into line of the press, etc.* (Wolfswinkel, 1994:35/36)

There were other clouds in the sky as well. All Jewish businesses had to be registered. Control over Jewish-led firms had to be handed over to German *Verwalter* (controller) – most of whom were crooks. This was the beginning of the systematic economic spoliation of the Jews.

Jews could no longer be blood donors, because Jewish blood should only run in Jewish veins. In coffee-bars and restaurants signs appeared with the text, *Forbidden for Jews*. In January 1941 cinemas closed their doors to them.

Groups of NSB men (members of the Dutch Nazi party) took to the streets in uniform and began terrorising Jewish neighbourhoods: attacking Jewish property, throwing stones at synagogues, forcing bar-owners to display signs saying *Forbidden for Jews* and provoking fights with Jews, for instance, by dragging them out of public transport. In general, the Jews tried to avoid confrontation, a well-tried formula from the diaspora.

Among Jews and non-Jews alike there was a naive belief that an attitude of cooperation would make things better. The decrees, although they took away one right after another, were tolerated not only because they were issued one by one, but because it was thought each one would be the last. It was the Germans' key strategy that no one ever knew where and when they would strike next. And every time, the German administration al-

Dutch Nazis began, like in Germany, to target Jewish shops

lowed the Jews to get used to the new situation, lulling them into believing the worst was over. Almost nobody foresaw that this system would ulti-mately lead to their complete destruction.

Even the ones who might have understood, like those who had lived through pogroms in Eastern Europe, did not want to acknowledge that the same thing was now happening in Holland, because there was nothing they could do about it.

*

However, there was a primitive form of resistance in response to the provocations of the Dutch National Socialists: young Jews banded together in gangs. One of the rare survivors told later of their experiences:

> One of us constructed some kind of assault-car, an old delivery-cart with a hood and two benches. When we got a call that Jews were being molested, off we went to fight back. (Mak, 1995:270, own translation)

The Nazi terror in the streets of Amsterdam caused serious rioting at the beginning of February 1941. One of the Dutch Nazis was killed in a street-brawl. The Germans decided to set an example and sealed off the Jewish neighbourhood. After another incident more than 400 'hostages'

Young Jews picked at random from the streets of Amsterdam on 22 February 1941. They were all sent to Mauthausen concentration camp; not one of them would come back

were arrested in a round-up (razzia). Ies Dikker, a haberdasher, was later to write from his hiding-place to his sister-in-law about the events he witnessed on the streets of Amsterdam:

> You will remember the neighbourhood on a Saturday afternoon. Women, men, boys, girls and children, all dressed to the nines. After a week of busy and hard work, finally the day of rest, the sabbath. Suddenly the lorries came rushing in and the whole neighbourhood was cordoned off. The bridges [over the canals] were drawn up and everybody was trapped. The streets were closed off and the Green Police could start its dreadful work. Soon screams of frightened girls and women were heard, the streets were filled with running men, who thought they could escape. They were the ones who got caught. Boys were torn away from their girlfriends and taken along; some people tried to hide in their houses, but were caught there and sometimes dragged down from the attics. Doors were kicked in and young people taken out. They were all taken to the Jonas Daniël Meijerplein, where they had to line up in front of the synagogue. (...) At the

smallest movement or the slightest sound a guard came and hit the offender
violently with his rifle or dropped its butt onto his feet. The lorries were on the
other side of the square and the brutes had the boys crawl to them on their knees.
(Dikker, 1995:31/32, own translation)

Indignation ran high among their fellow-citizens: these people were innocent! The politically very active Jewish labour movement enjoyed much
sympathy and solidarity in other parts of the city. Pamphlets passed from
hand to hand, calling upon the people of Amsterdam to mount a protest
strike. A large percentage of the workers responded to the appeal by the
illegal Communist Party to strike as an answer to these razzias (round-ups).
One of the organisers looks back to the meeting on the day before the strike
20 years later:

> ...we told them [those present at the meeting] that what was happening in
> Germany could maybe take place over there and that was their business, but that
> we as the people from Amsterdam (...) had played with our Jewish friends and
> Jewish girlfriends from when we were small, together in the same street, and on
> the same staircases of the same houses. We could not tolerate this, we had to do
> everything possible to bring Amsterdam to a standstill the next day. (De Jong,
> 1966:162, own translation)

The next day – the 25th of February – Amsterdam did come to a standstill.
The strike began among the public transport workers: hardly one tram left
its depot that morning. From there, it spread to the docks and the steel
factories in the harbour. Other factories, some outside Amsterdam, followed. The strike was a complete success.

The Germans were taken by surprise, but retaliated almost immediately.
After two days the strike tapered off. Shortly before, the Jewish community
had had to agree to the establishment of a *Joodsche Raad* (Jewish Council),
which had to cooperate closely with the Germans. It would be held responsible for the proper execution of German demands.[2]

The Council was composed of prominent people from the Jewish community. It started with a board of twenty members, but its staff quickly
expanded. At the height of its activities, more than 17,000 employees were
working for the Council. It was assigned the task of maintaining order and
passing on German commands to the entire Jewish population of Amsterdam. By engaging the Jews in their own persecution and by playing them
off against each other, the German authorities managed to have everything
running smoothly and efficiently. The dismissed president judge of the
Supreme Court, L.E. Visser, was one of the first to see through the German
intentions. This Jewish Council could, according to him, be nothing else but
a willing tool in the hands of the Nazis.

The two chairmen of the Jewish Council, diamond-trader Abraham
Asscher and Professor of Ancient History David Cohen, sincerely believed,
however, that they would best serve the interests of the Jewish community

Jewish children at the edge of their neighbourhood: "the grass is always greener..."

by cooperating with the Germans. Cohen was later to write in his memoirs that the Jewish Council wanted to be a dividing wall between the Jews and the Germans. In 1990, his son, Herman Cohen, wrote in an article how little

discussion his father's chairmanship of the Jewish Council had caused at
home:

> I can imagine I may have heard about the existence of the 'Joodsche Raad'
> without giving it any further thought, just because my father was in charge of
> it. He had always been in charge of something, for as long as I can remember.
> Always and everywhere respected and valued for his judgment, dedication and
> integrity. When I left Holland in 1939 [Herman Cohen went to Israel] he had
> been chairman of the Committee for German Refugees for six years and the
> leading figure in the Committee for Special Jewish Interests (...). Why should he
> now not have been chairman of a similar committee (...) where he would again
> stand up for the interests of a threatened Jewish community? (Cohen in *Jaarboek
> RIOD II*, 1990:115/116, own translation)

With hindsight, it is easy to be scathing and critical about the patterns of
behaviour of the Joodsche Raad. Nevertheless, it is hard to see how Herzberg's judgment can be faulted when he compares the activities of the
Council to that of a firm of undertakers:

> They have presumably laboured under the fiction that they could accomplish
> something by deftly manoeuvring, or 'preventing worse', as the term went, or
> delaying the execution of the decrees. Now we know the truth. The Jewish
> Councils were nothing more than undertakers, deemed necessary by the Third
> Reich to bury doomed and executed Jewish communities. (...) And as such the
> Jewish Councils have done their job excellently. They only made one mistake:
> they had the illusion that the undertaker can make a deal with death. Nothing
> is further from the truth. Death is implacable, pitiless. (Herzberg, 1950:30/31,
> own translation)

The strike of February 1941, one of the few spontaneous mass protests in
German-occupied Europe, expressed the Dutch revulsion at Nazi repression and persecution of the Jews. This does not mean every Dutchman was
a friend of the Jews, merely that they did not like German interference in
domestic affairs. The well-known slogan, *Keep your dirty hands off our dirty
Jews*, expresses this sentiment aptly.

Almost all of the 400 hostages were dead before the autumn of 1941. They
had been taken to Mauthausen concentration camp in Austria and murdered there. It was at that time the most notorious concentration camp, with
a commandant who gave to his son as a birthday present 'fifty Jews for
execution'. Families of the hostages were notified that their perfectly
healthy loved ones had died of *Herzversagen* (heart failure) or some other
deadly disease like sunstroke.

*

Up to this point, Seyss-Inquart had remained silent on the so-called Jewish question.[3] Annoyed by the events in Amsterdam, he announced the total segregation of Jews from social and economic life: *We will hit the Jews where we find them and whoever takes their side will have to bear the consequences.* This was – in March 1941 – shortly after the first executions of Dutchmen who were accused of resistance activities, among them two Jews who had been involved in the street riots in Amsterdam.

In the wake of the policy to subordinate the Dutch people to Nazi rule, the persecution of the Jews intensified. Many decrees were issued, varying from small torments like a prohibition on keeping pigeons or observing Jewish holidays to the expropriation of Jewish possessions. The net closed a little more every week.

The organisation of this policy was entrusted to the *Zentralstelle für Jüdische Auswanderung* (Central Bureau for Jewish Emigration) in Amsterdam, whose immediate head was SS-Hauptsturmführer Ferdinand Aus der Fünten. Similar offices were functioning in Berlin, Vienna and Prague. The name of this organisation originally inspired some hope. It seemed to indicate that the Germans were still considering emigration as a 'solution to the Jewish problem'. After the invasion of the Soviet Union in June 1941, Reichsmarschall Hermann Goering ordered Reinhard Heydrich, Chief of the German Security Police, to draw up plans for the *Gesamtlösung* ('Comprehensive Solution'). In the autumn of 1941, these plans gradually took shape; during the war on the Eastern Front, it was found that mass destruction of humans was possible. The term 'Final Solution' was not used yet: Hitler was still said to be looking at *Aussiedlung* (relocation) of the Jews.

The Germans continued to carry out their policies of separating Jews and non-Jews. In Holland from 1 May 1941 onwards, Jews were excluded from certain professions, such as physician, dentist, pharmacist or lawyer. They were also debarred from the stock-exchange. And in the spring and summer of 1941, a number of decrees forbade Jews to attend public meetings, exhibitions or concerts, visit museums, public parks or zoos, cafes and restaurants, use sleeping and dining cars on trains, go to sporting events, make use of swimming pools and public libraries, visit markets and auctions. When access to the North Sea beaches was prohibited, the NSB newspaper wrote: *Our North Sea will no longer serve to rinse down fat Jewish bodies.*

The exclusion – after the summer holidays of 1941 – of Jewish pupils and students from schools and universities hit very hard. Jewish children had to go to Jewish schools where they were taught by Jewish teachers, a form of segregation that was gradually introduced in all spheres of social life. A small boy in one of the northern provinces was told by his mother:

"Benjamin, listen! I have to tell you something serious: you cannot go to your school any more!" Well, that didn't seem so serious to me. Every day off from

After September 1941, Jewish children had to attend schools "for Jews only"

school, I liked that. But that was not what they had in mind. "No," my mother said, "you have to go to a different school now. The Germans don't want Jewish children to go to the same schools as other children any more. You have to go to a Jewish school." But I did not want that at all. I wanted to stay with my friends. "But we are not different!" I said to my mother. "That is what you think, but the Germans think differently." I had no choice. I had to go to the Jewish school. It was on the other side of our town. No, I did not like it, especially since we often had fights with other children, NSB-children, who provoked us. They called us 'dirty Jews'. I began to play truant a lot. (*Westerbork cahiers* 3, 1994:23, own translation)

Some Jewish teachers who had been dismissed in November 1941 now found employment at the newly created Jewish schools. Historian Jacques Presser tried to keep up the spirits of the children: *Children, we are all in the same boat. They tell us we are inferior, but we will show them we are* not. (Bregstein, 1972:88, own translation)

Jewish religious life – traditionally with an important social dimension – became increasingly difficult. Jewish libraries were closed down and sealed off. Admission to the sources of Jewish culture, like the house of Spinoza, was prohibited. All traces of Jewish life in the Netherlands had to be eradicated. Names of streets and squares – commemorating famous Dutchmen of Jewish origin – were rebaptised in National-Socialist fashion, sometimes causing grim jokes. The confiscation of the libraries made such an impression that some compared it to the taking of the Ark of the Covenant by the Philistines.

As in other occupied countries, the Nazis transferred books, antique furniture, and art collections to Germany. This was done by the *Einsatzstab Rosenberg*, the head of which was the Nazi ideologist Alfred Rosenberg. Reichsmarschall Hermann Goering also was a notorious collector of art and travelled through the whole of Europe to enlarge his collection, which he claimed was the largest art collection in Europe owned by an individual.

As with the separate Jewish schools, the Dutch also had to become familiar with a separate Jewish Symphony Orchestra, a Jewish cabaret ensemble, a Jewish theatre company, all performing in the *Hollandsche Schouwburg* (Dutch Theatre), which was now renamed the *Joodsche Schouwburg* (Jewish Theatre). All these were to be short-lived. No non-Jewish audiences were allowed. Works of Jewish composers, like Mendelssohn and Mahler, could no longer be performed by non-Jewish orchestras. It was not always clear, however, who was considered Jewish and who was not, as in the case of the French composer Saint-Saëns. Sometimes, illegal concerts or plays were organised in the homes of private people, on behalf of disadvantaged Jewish artists, but these expressions of solidarity remained rare.

The majority of the Dutch responded with indifference to all these measures and decrees. Only the Roman Catholic and Orthodox Protestant churches communicated their disagreement with the discriminatory policy of the Germans from the pulpit and in pastoral letters. Conversely, the Dutch civil authorities were too often more than loyal in the execution of the many decrees. After the war a civil servant testified before the Parliamentary Committee of Inquiry and said: *Often one made an effort to be ahead of the Germans, in order to do what one supposed the Germans would do, at least what one supposed the Germans would like.*

Even the mouthpieces of the resistance – the underground press that had sprung up after the German invasion – seemed initially hardly interested in the measures taken against their Jewish fellow citizens. Predominantly, they published news from the war fronts which did not appear in the German-controlled regular press; they encouraged people and made appeal after appeal not to cooperate with the Germans. In the novel *Verduisterde jaren* (Darkened Years) by S. de Vries Jr., it is said about this underground press that no matter how hard the Germans tried to stop these publications, they kept on appearing:

The Germans had demanded all lettertypes from all printing firms in Holland. These they had been given, but the underground press continued to publish excellent papers. Many editors were caught and then the headlines in the [legal] papers said: "Condemned to Death!" But the torch was always carried further. New editors were found. Always new men were prepared to see to it that the clandestine papers came out. And they became better all the time in lay-out, spelling and printing. (De Vries, 1945:81, own translation)

It is estimated that Holland with its more than 1200 underground presses had the highest number of 'illegal' newspapers.

For those who wanted to see, however, there were unmistakable signs pointing in the direction of an approaching catastrophe. After the razzias in February in Amsterdam, quite a few more had taken place, allegedly as deeds of reprisal for sabotage. In June 1941, 300 Jews, most of them high school pupils who had worked in the Jewish labour village of Wieringermeer before the war, were sent to Mauthausen. Abel Herzberg, the director of the village, wrote in a letter: *Optimism is one hundred times another word for negligence, self-deceit, unpreparedness.*

On 22 October 1941, a decree forbade non-Jews to do household work in Jewish homes, because of the alleged moral and sexual risks 'Aryan' girls were taking. 'Race violation' the Germans called it. A couple of months later, in March 1942, Jews were prohibited to have sexual contact with non-Jews. 'Interracial' marriages were forbidden. Racial hygiene was not limited to contact between Jews and non-Jews. Blacks from the Dutch West Indies, for instance, were no longer allowed to perform in the jazz joints of Amsterdam. According to the Dutch authorities, negroes from Surinam would weaken the existing revulsion towards blacks among white women with their sensual music.

The racist policies of the Nazis obviously affected all kinds of aspects of Dutch cultural and communal life. Jews were excluded from participation in non-profit-making associations and companies other than those run by Jews and for Jews. This was a severe blow since Jews played a very important role in many Dutch institutions and public associations.

Soon, the Germans drastically threatened the basic economic survival of the Jews. Most Jews were out of work by the autumn of 1941. Ies Dikker, for instance, had had to close down his haberdashery by order of the German authorities. He described his experiences in a long letter to his sister-in-law, who had emigrated to South America:

You will wonder what we lived on. The shop closed, no source of income. We were not allowed to have money; gold, silver, diamonds, and so on had to be handed in. What did we have left to exist on? You should also know there was a special bank that confiscated Jewish properties: Lippman, Rosenthal & Co. Of course the Jewish directors had been fired; there were just NSB'ers working. We were only allowed two hundred and fifty guilders in cash, the rest was confiscated. Millions have been put into that bank, millions have not. Most Jews had Christian friends, willing to keep money and valuables. Those were more numerous then than when they were needed to protect our lives, but it was of course less dangerous and much more profitable. Because it is certain that there are still a lot of treasures hidden with many people, and I am sure that much has been stolen – on purpose (...) Some months ago I read in an underground paper that the Lippman-Rosenthal bank was liquidated. Gone are the jewellery and the millions! (Dikker, 1995:61, own translation)

In the autumn of 1941, anti-Jewish violence spilled over into the other provinces of Holland. Forced removals from their houses and internments began, particularly of German Jews. German Jews had been deprived of their German citizenship in 1941, and at the end of that year many of them had to report for *voluntary emigration*, one of the many writings on the wall. They were sent directly to the concentration camp of Westerbork in the northeast of Holland. This camp had been enlarged by orders of Seyss-Inquart into a 'refugee camp' for German-Jewish emigrants.

But also the unemployed Dutch Jews were placed into one of the forced labour camps. Thousands of Jews became familiar with the sadism of members of the NSB (Dutch Nazi Party) and the Dutch SS, who acted as camp guards. In 1942, thousands of Dutch Jews were taken from the labour camps to Westerbork as well.

At the beginning of 1942, the Germans began concentrating Jews into Amsterdam.[4] Moving was prohibited, except to Amsterdam. They were forced out of other cities and villages, and whole provinces became prohibited areas. In *Bitter Herbs*, Marga Minco describes how the parents of her main character have to leave their house in Amersfoort and move to Amsterdam.

Labour camps and evacuation caused great hardship in the first half of 1942, but few recognised the real nature of these fatal steps as they led towards the final catastrophe.

*

Other major annoyances were still tot follow. By March 1942 Jews were no longer allowed to use private motor vehicles. During funerals, only the corpse could be moved by car; the mourners had to walk. Jews were excluded from non-Jewish hairdressers and pedicurists, and they were denied the use of pubiic telephones – private Jewish subscribers had their telephones disconnected.

Still it was not enough.

Esther van Vriesland, a 15-year-old girl from Gorcum, wrote in her diary on 14 June 1942:

We were still in bed yesterday, when mother came with the newspaper. There were all sorts of new regulations: no more canoeing, rowing, swimming and fishing. In one word: awful. How to spend the holiday now? Bicycles have to be handed in. This I don't mind too much. I don't feel like a holiday at all any more. I looked forward to the holidays so much! Horrid, that's what it is. (Van Vriesland, 1990:123, own translation)

On 30 June she writes:

> I am so terribly miserable. New regulation: we can't go out after eight o' clock
> at night till six in the morning. Shopping between three and five in the afternoon.
> Holding of certain professions forbidden, no more public transport, so from now
> on we have to walk... And for persons with a travel permit: wait until everybody
> else is in the train and only sit down when all non-Jews have found a seat.
> Otherwise stand up. O God, how humiliating. When I heard about it for the first
> time I could have cried. Even now, but then I felt so rebellious. Will it never end?
> Is there no God? (Van Vriesland, 1990:129, own translation)

Just three months later Esther was gassed in Auschwitz. The last line in her
diary: *Please, let me write about peace in the next notebook.*

Anne Frank, about the same age as Esther van Vriesland, writes in her
diary on 30 June 1942 that a friend of hers used to say: *I am scared to do
anything these days, because I am afraid it might be forbidden.*[5]

And it took 16-year-old Moshe Flinker one-and-a-half hours to get to
school in July of that same year: his bicycle had become the property of the
Reich, and Jews could no longer use public transport. It was the last day of
school before the summer holidays, he heard he had passed his end-of-year
exams, but he did not know he would never go back to school.

*

A most serious step to the final act was the introduction of the Yellow Star.
Early in May 1942, Jews were required to wear a prominent yellow star on
their clothes in public. It was a symbol borrowed from the Middle Ages,
like the triangular Jewish hat Jews were required to wear in eighteenth-cen-
tury Venice. It was a black, six-pointed Star of David on yellow cloth with
the word *JOOD* (JEW) written on it. People had to buy the stars from the
Jewish Council. On May 21 *Het Joodsche Weekblad* (The Jewish Weekly)
warned that any infringement of the new regulations concerning the
Yellow Star could have *very serious consequences*. The same issue of The
Jewish Weekly contained fifteen announcements of engagements, seven
of weddings, four of births and seven of barmitzvahs.[6] German intentions
were obvious: branding Jews publicly like this, they hoped to bring about
a visible distinction that would lead to further isolation, humiliation and
insecurity.

Responses varied. Should one wear the star with pride, as Robert
Weltsch, editor of the German Zionist paper, *Jüdische Rundschau*, suggested
already in 1933: *Wear It with Pride, The Yellow Badge*. One of the two
chairmen of the Jewish Council, Professor Cohen, literally said the same
thing to SS-Hauptsturmführer Aus der Fünten. Many, however, realised
that the introduction of the star served as a symbol for the persecutions as
a whole: the visualising of the demon. Some of them who opposed, like the

son of the above-mentioned judge L.E. Visser, paid with their life for this act of defiance.

Soon some ordinary Dutchmen would start betraying Jews for not wearing it, although in the beginning a few non-Jews pinned one on their own clothes as a sign of solidarity or offered Jews their seat in a tram or train. However, it should have been clear that a new phase in the persecution was imminent, the phase of deportations – *'emigration'* in the veiled jargon of the Nazis.

In *Bitter Herbs*, Marga Minco writes about the day her father brought the yellow stars home with him, and the family sat down at the table to sew the stars onto their clothes. First there was a discussion about whether they would look nice or not, then about the colour cotton they should use, the colour of the star or the colour of the garment. She continues:

> We fetched our coats from the hallstand and got down to sewing stars on them. My sister Betty did it very carefully, with small, invisible stitches. "You must hem them," she said, when she saw how I was fixing the star on my coat with big, untidy stitches. "That looks much neater." "I think they're such awkward things to sew on," I complained. "How on earth can you get a hem round those beastly points?" (Minco, 1960:15)

Her mother was pleased her father had brought so many: *"It's certainly convenient,"* she said. *"Now we can keep some in reserve for our summer clothes."*

Fifty years later the historian of the Dutch Jewry, Jaap Meijer wrote this little poem:

Sternstunde (Hour of the Star)

To have worn
a star once
They can never
take that away from me. (own translation)

Segregation and isolation of the Jews were complete by the middle of 1942. Jews were by now absolutely powerless. They could only be further badgered, imprisoned and ... deported.

Anne Frank

When the German armies occupied Holland, Anne Frank was one month away from her eleventh birthday. After the family moved to Amsterdam, the life of Anne and her sister Margot had become like the life of so many other Dutch children of that same age. We know that Anne was a very lively child, attractive, not pretty – like her sister Margot – and that she had many friends. Miep Gies remembers one of the first times – in 1937 – that she met Anne:

> She was now eight years old, still somewhat thin and delicate, but with electric grey-green eyes, with green flecks. Her eyes were very deeply set, so that when they were half-closed they looked as if they were shrouded in dark shade. Anne had her mother's nose and her father's mouth, but with a slight overbite and cleft chin.(...) Margot was ten years old, very pretty, also with shiny dark hair. Both girls had their hair cut just below their ears, parted on the side, held back by a barrette. Margot's eyes were dark. She was shy and quiet with us, and very, very well-mannered, as was little Anne.(...) Both girls spoke perfect Dutch. (Gies, 1987:23)

Anne liked to be the centre of attention. Her childhood friend Hannah Goslar, herself a refugee from Berlin, tells how at school Anne would always be surrounded by friends. Later, while in hiding, Anne would look back upon those years with a mixture of nostalgia and amazement; she wrote on 7 March 1944:

> If I think now of my life in 1942, it all seems so unreal. It was quite a different Anne who enjoyed that heavenly existence from the Anne who has grown wise within these walls. Yes, it was a heavenly life. Boy friends at every turn, about twenty friends and acquaintances of my own age, the darling of nearly all the teachers, spoilt from top to toe by Mummy and Daddy, lots of sweets, enough pocket money, what more could one want? (...) All the teachers were entertained by my cute answers, my amusing remarks, my smiling face, and my questioning looks. That is all I was – a terrible flirt, coquettish and amusing.(...) Now I look back at that Anne as an amusing, but very superficial girl, who has nothing to do with the Anne of today. (Frank, 1995:146)

It was the academic year – September 1941 to July 1942 – when she had had to leave her Montessori school and go to the specially created 'Jewish Lyceum'. In the diary which she received on her thirteenth birthday (12 June 1942), she speaks of her everyday anxieties – passing the end-of-year exams, *dates with boys – but surprisingly little about the number of decrees that are limiting Jewish life more and more. She lists a number of them on 20 June 1942, but remarks casually in the same breath:*

> *So we could not do this and were forbidden to do that. But life went on in spite of it all.*

When she wrote those words down, she did not know that less than three weeks later life would come to a complete stop, at least that kind of life. On 5 July 1942 her sister Margot received orders to report for transport to a labour camp in the East. Anne writes: Margot is sixteen; would they really take girls of that age away alone? She was probably unaware that her father had been preparing for exactly an occasion like this for over a year. The laboratory behind his office had not been used for some time, and Otto Frank had adopted the habit of taking something with him from home every time he went to his office. But he needed promises of help from people who would look after them. He had approached Miep Gies:

> *"Miep," he said, "Edith, Margot, Anne and I are planning to go under, to go into hiding." (...) "As you will be working on as usual right next to us, I need to know if you have any objections?" I told him I did not. He took a breath and asked, "Miep, are you willing to take on the responsibility of taking care of us while we are in hiding?" "Of course," I answered. There is a look between two people once or twice in a lifetime that cannot be described by words. That look passed between us. "Miep, for those who help Jews the punishment is harsh, imprisonment, perhaps..." I cut him off. I said, "Of course, I meant it." (Gies, 1987:64)*

On 9 July 1942, the Frank family disappeared from view.

III
Deportation or into Hiding

This is not time for poetry. (Moshe Flinker, January 19, 1943)

Today many of those who once laughed, do not laugh anymore. (Speech by Hitler, November 8, 1942)

On 20 January 1942 in a villa in the Berlin suburb of Wannsee, 15 high dignitaries of the Third Reich gathered under the chairmanship of Reinhard Heydrich. They met for about one and a half hours. Their aim was to discuss the organisation of the biggest genocide of this century: the murder of the Jews of Europe, or in the German jargon of that time, *die Endlösung der Judenfrage* (the Final Solution of the Jewish Problem). SS-Obersturmbannführer Adolf Eichmann, who compiled the Wannsee Conference Protocols and would later organise the deportations of the European Jews to the death camps, recalled during his trial in Jerusalem three decades later:

> At the end, Heydrich was smoking and drinking brandy in a corner near a stove. We all sat together like comrades...not to talk shop, but to rest after long hours of work.

The fate of six million Jews was sealed in one and a half hours, by people who met in the congenial atmosphere of a warm fire, brandy and good cigars, like a reunion of old comrades. Almost immediately after German forces had invaded the Soviet Union on 22 June 1941, the systematic murder of Eastern European Jews began behind the front lines. The so-called *Kommissarbefehl* (Commissars' Order) signalled the killing of as many 'enemies of the Reich' as possible, initially political officers of the Red Army, but later extended to all partisans and Jews.

Specially designated mobile killing squads, the *Einsatzgruppen*, shot 33,771 Jews in two days at the end of September in a ravine called Babi Yar, near Kiev. Small-scale Babi Yars occurred almost daily behind the advancing German armies in many places for many months. Almost 2 million Jews lost their lives behind the front lines of Nazi-occupied Poland, the Baltic States and the Soviet Union.

With the coordination of the murder of all European Jews, every pretense of looking for other solutions disappeared: from the autumn of 1941 onwards all other plans, e.g. emigration and/or resettlement in the East, were shelved.

The killing of 11 million European Jews, the estimated figure given to the participants of the Wannsee Conference, which included the Jews of Britain, Ireland, Sweden and other still unoccupied countries of Europe, would place a heavy logistical burden on many ministeries and government departments, and in particular the railways. Therefore, it was decided to transport the Jews with *Sonderzüge* (special trains) to the gas chambers of the extermination camps, all of them located on a main railroad line in Poland. These were existing, purpose-built camps, like Belzec and Majdanek, or new ones which would soon be under construction, like Birkenau (or Auschwitz II), Treblinka and Sobibor. The words used on paper were deceiving: 'evacuation' or 'emigration', never extermination or destruction. No matter how openly persecution and expulsion had occurred until now, the last act was to take place in the greatest secrecy: Hitler, Himmler and Heydrich, like their organisers and executioners, knew only too well they would never find approval from large parts of the population for this policy.

Deception, like the use of these euphemisms, was therefore applied systematically by the Nazis, especially when it concerned the Jews of Western Europe. There they wished to avoid at all costs heart-rending scenes such as had taken place in the ghettos and country villages of Eastern Europe, where often parents had had to be separated forcefully from their children. They were prepared to go to great lengths not to upset the rest of the population. Deception, even to the very end of the road. At the little station of Treblinka, for instance, there were fake ticketbooths (as if one could buy a return ticket), fake 1st and 2nd class waiting-rooms, fake toilets, etc. The façade was maintained that the Jews of Western Europe were 'to be put to work'. Many Jews and non-Jews believed it, wanted to believe it, because it was the only thing that made sense. The alternative – a mass murder of unprecedented proportions – was too grotesque to be considered seriously.[1]

About one month after the Wannsee conference, the first trains came to Poland from the occupied territories in the West. In previous years, the Nazis had gained experience during the 'Euthanasia' program: at least 70,000 mentally or physically handicapped men, women and children had been put to death. Specialists were developing an improved killer gas, Zyklon-B, that presented new standards of speed and efficiency for the killing process. The Zyklon-B gas made it possible to destroy (in German: *vernichten*) ever greater numbers of Jews at much greater speed, in a true assembly-line manner.

Hitler had used the term 'Vernichtung' literally in a speech before the Reichstag (German Parliament) as early as 30 January 1939:

Wenn es dem internationalen Finanzjudentum in und ausserhalb Europas gelingen sollte die Völker noch einmal in einen Weltkrieg zu stürzen, dan wird das Ergebnis nicht Bolschewiserung der Erde und damit der Sieg des Judentums sein, sondern die Vernichtung der jüdischen Rasse in Europa. ("If international finance Jewry within Europe and abroad should succeed once more in plunging the people into a world war, then the consequence will be not the Bolshevization of the world and therewith a victory of Jewry, but on the contrary, the destruction of the Jewish race in Europe.")

His words were greeted with thunderous applause. In a little-known speech of 8 March 1939, Hitler even said that, once France and Great Britain were defeated, the *Dollar Juden* of the USA would also have to be conquered.[2] And in his speech at the Sports Palace in Berlin on 30 January 1942, ten days after the Wannsee Conference, Hitler declared that his prophetic statement of the 30 January 1939 about *die Vernichtung des Judentums* ('Destruction of Jewry') was now about to become reality. The whole of Europe was to be made *Judenrein* ('free of Jews'): *The result of this war will be the complete annihilation of the Jews.*

*

In a letter to Seyss-Inquart of August 1941, the highest SS official in Holland, Hanns Albin Rauter, was already using the phrase: *die kommende Endlösung der Judenfrage* ('the coming Final Solution'). Rauter[3] set up office in The Hague, assisted by Dr Wilhelm Harster, chief of the Security Police, and a representative of Adolf Eichmann, Wilhelm Zöpf. Three months after using this phrase, Rauter asked the Dutch secretary-general of Home Affairs what would happen if he, Rauter, were to have all Dutch Jews deported to Poland. The secretary-general answered that in that case he and his colleagues would certainly step down, and the majority of the civil servants would follow this example. *In that case the Germans had to manage for themselves*, he said. The Germans managed, not in the least thanks to the cooperation of the Dutch authorities and the Jewish Council.

Since it was obviously impossible to kill all of the Jews at the same time, the SS authorities in Berlin decided Holland had to supply about a thousand every week. At that rate it would have taken the Germans just under three years to transport 140,000 Jews from Holland to their ultimate destiny in Poland.

On 26 June 1942, representatives of the Jewish Council in Amsterdam were told that Jewish men and women between the ages of 16 and 40 would be put to work in Germany *under police protection*. On Sunday, 5 July 1942, the first groups were called up via a special mail delivery. One of those who received such a letter was Margot Frank, Anne's older sister. It was the sign for the family to go into hiding almost immediately. On 8 July 1942, Anne wrote in her new diary, a present from her father for her 13th birthday on 12 June:

> Into hiding – where would we go, in a town or the country, in a house or a cottage, when, how, where...? These were questions I was not allowed to ask, but I couldn't get them out of my mind. (Frank, 1995: 12)

The call-ups caused great upheavals in Amsterdam: Presser tells the story of some students of the Jewish Lyceum who also received their call-up card. Suddenly, a girl from the highest form stood up. She and her sister had both been called up. What should they do? One of her teachers (Jacques Presser himself) later described their dismay:

> There she was, this girl of seventeen years old, with her matriculation certificate full of A's, completely alone, unprotected, but upright in front of that green table behind which her teachers sat. The historian, writing this down after so many years, still sees her standing there, a nice, intelligent girl, thoroughly decent; he stills hears her question, has never been able to forget it: 'Ladies and gentlemen, please tell us what we must do.' One of us responded immediately: 'Don't go!' Another one agreed, and another one, and one more. The others remained silent, one bowed his head. Nobody could really help them – and so they went to their death. (Presser I, 1965:255, own translation)

Obviously, everyone tried their best to avoid the transports leaving for the labour camps in the East with monotonous regularity after that first transport of July 1942. Although very few expected to be killed there, it was still considered better to stay in Holland, together with relatives and friends. Often the resistance to being sent on a transport would crumble once family and friends had been deported. Initially, many people managed to get a *Sperre*, an exemption from removal to the Westerbork transit camp, because they had an important position within the Jewish community or were employed in vital industries for the German war machine. Baptised Jews and Jews in mixed marriages (i.e. Jews married to 'Aryans') also received a *Sperre*,[4] at least temporarily. The *Sperre* was yet another example of the way in which the Nazis played their cat-and-mouse game with the Jews. In the beginning the German police authorities could afford to be generous with the handing out of *Sperre*: the supply of unprotected Jews was still plentiful. However, as this supply ran out and Jews were less and less inclined to register voluntarily for deportation, many *Sperren* collapsed.[5] In the end only the Jews deemed most vital to the German aims still had one. The desperate scramble to obtain an exemption from deportation led to the birth of many dubious and shady schemes and lists. The most famous of these was the so-called Weinreb list. Friedrich Weinreb, an economist from The Hague, played a game of deceit and fraud with the German SD (Sicherheitsdienst = Security Police): at stake were the lives of more than six hundred Jews, who had paid for a place on his list. With the cooperation of a non-existent general in Berlin, Weinreb claimed these Jews were awaiting emigration, which would bring in much-needed foreign exchange for the German Reich. In the end, the charade was exposed. Weinreb managed to go into hiding, but most of the Jews on his list were arrested and deported.

*

On 9 July 1942 the Jewish Symphony Orchestra gave its twenty-fifth concert and the programme fittingly included Saint Saëns' *Danse Macabre*. On 14 July 1942 the first train left Amsterdam for Westerbork with 962 people. And one day later, the first consignment of 1135 people, mainly German Jews, left Westerbork and were taken to Auschwitz. From then on, on nearly every Tuesday morning for two long years, a transport train would leave Westerbork. The great majority of them were destined for Auschwitz, but approximately 34,000 went to Sobibor in Poland and several thousands to Bergen-Belsen in Germany or Theresienstadt in Czechoslovakia. In contrast to Belgium and France, the transports from Holland continued almost uninterrupted from July 1942 to September 1944.

Etty Hillesum, who worked for the Jewish Council in Amsterdam for a few months, saw the desperate efforts of many people who tried to avoid deportation. How, she asked herself, would she react to the same fate many others had to undergo:

> I feel deep moral indignation at a regime that treats human beings in such a way. But events have become too overwhelming and too demonic to be stemmed with personal resentment and bitterness.(...) People often get worked up when I say it doesn't really matter whether I go or somebody else does, the main thing is that so many thousands have to go. (...) I don't think I would feel happy if I were exempted from what so many others have to suffer. I know that whatever I may have to give to others, I can give it no matter where I am, here in the circle of my friends or over there, in a concentration camp. And it is sheer arrogance to think oneself too good to share the fate of the masses. (Hillesum, 1983:150)

Before the first deportation, Jews were strongly urged by the Jewish Council to present themselves on time at the railway station for transport to Westerbork. About 50% did not appear at the appointed time. The Germans responded angrily. Jews would from now on be rounded up from their houses at night. Dutch policemen would be in charge. The rest of the Dutch population were to notice as little as possible of what was going on. Call-ups, razzias and transports followed in quick succession. A Jewish woman wrote about a visit to her parents:

> Shaking with horror, mother told how she would sit in the dark in front of her window every night, while all around her people were being dragged from their houses like animals. She was rigid with fear, because it could be her and father's turn any moment. How down in the street the big lorries had stood, full of people crying and screaming with fear, of whom she could see only the confused tumble of legs... (Presser I, 1965:281, own translation)

The physicist Jona Oberski, then a boy of not yet 5 years old, describes in a book called *Childhood* how he was put on a transport with his parents:

A man was shouting. I woke up. The door of my room was pulled open. Somebody clumped in. The light went on. "What's in here?" the man yelled. My mother came in. "That's my little boy," she said. "Go away, I'll attend to him myself."

"Hurry, hurry," the man yelled. My mother came over and patted me on the head. I kept my eyes shut. "Wake up, angel, we have to take a trip. Remember? We told you we might have to go away again. And now it's happened. Be a good boy. Dress yourself, the way you always do."

"Hurry, hurry," the man yelled. (Oberski, 1983:27)

As stated before, from September 1942, Jews were collected every night from their houses. History teacher Presser would later describe how pupils would disappear from his class on a regular basis and how other pupils would communicate this:

I would enter the classroom, again there was one missing. The children answered with gestures. There were two gestures, one meant: caught. The other one: gone into hiding. Never a word was spoken during this ritual. (Bregstein, 1981:41-43, own translation)

In November 1942 more than 2000 Jews were rounded up in Amsterdam. Did they know what was in store for them? On 9 October 1942, Anne Frank makes a remark in her diary, which seems significant and is often quoted:

Our many Jewish friends are being taken away by the dozen. These people are treated by the Gestapo without a shred of decency, being loaded into cattle trucks and sent to Westerbork, the big Jewish camp in Drente. Westerbork sounds terrible...If it is as bad as this in Holland, whatever will it be like in the distant and barbarous regions they are sent to? We assume that most of them are murdered. The English radio speaks of their being gassed; perhaps that is the quickest way to die.

On the other hand, most people were inclined to assume they were dealing with an isolated incident when confronted with a travesty of justice. They could not believe or imagine that the murder of millions of people was the rule and not the exception. Of course, they saw with their own eyes that the Nazis killed political opponents and Jews everywhere, but nobody could imagine in those first years of the war that they were out to systematically kill all the Jews.

On 2 August 1942 a political staff member of Reichskommissar Seyss-Inquart called the Jews *the biggest enemy of Germany* and announced that they would be sent eastwards *just as poor and full of lice* as they had come to the West hundreds of years earlier. *They are in for difficult times*, the German concluded his speech. He was widely quoted in the Dutch press, and many

Jews understood the consequences. One Dutch Jew, for instance, tried to be exempted from deportation by appealing to the commander of the Wehrmacht in Holland, General Friedrich Christiansen. In a letter he pointed out that he was wounded when fighting in May 1940, having lost his right leg and his left foot. Christiansen himself wrote on top of the letter, before he sent it on: *a Jew is a Jew, legs or no legs.*

Others tried to escape to countries where they would be safer. Often those attempts failed because of betrayal. The physician Elie Cohen remembered 20 years later:

> I was brought to concentration camp Amersfoort, because four Dutchmen had offered to take me and my family to Sweden for the amount of thirteen thousand Dutch guilders. We accepted this offer, but instead of being taken to the promised cargo boat in Delfzijl, we were handed over to the SD-man Schröder in front of the station of Groningen.[6] (De Jong, 1966:627, own translation)

Those who tried to escape had to face grave perils, like 16-year-old Moshe Flinker, who fled with his family to Belgium.

> Early next morning my father sent three women to The Hague to escort my mother, brother and sisters to Roosendaal. Travelling by train was then most dangerous because it was forbidden by the Germans: if anyone dared travel and got caught, he was sent to one of the concentration camps which no one could hope to leave alive. The feat was difficult from another point of view, too, for our family consists of nine people: my father and mother, my five sisters, my small brother, and myself. (Flinker, 1965:21/22)

In three consecutive nights following their arrival in Roosendaal, the family crossed the border into Belgium, except his youngest sister: she arrived 10 days later.

In Belgium things were not as strict as they were in Holland. There, as in France, the Germans had set up military administrations to which the local civilian authority had been made subservient. In Holland, on the other hand, the Germans had established a civilian administration which included German officials and local collaborators. This civilian administration left more room for the SS to determine policy towards the Jews and greater authority to execute it. Because of the SS regime in Holland and the very loyal attitude of Jews and non-Jews alike, only 25% of Dutch Jewry would survive the war in contrast to Belgium where 60% of all Jews survived[7], and in France and Italy where 75% to 85%, respectively, survived.

Neutral countries like Switzerland, Sweden or Portugal were, of course, safer. From there, the fugitive could try and reach England. An estimated 3000 Dutch Jews were successful in escaping this way, most of them young single men. The Seventh Day Adventist Jean Weidner managed to bring to safety almost 250 Dutchmen thanks to his escape organisation *Dutch-Paris.*

His rescue network included people who forged papers, found shelters and escorted fugitives across borders. An illustration of the risks involved is the case of Suzy Kraay. She was arrested in Paris carrying an address book with names of network contacts. As she was being taken to police headquarters, she managed to drop it on the sidewalk. A courteous Frenchman picked it up and returned it to her. As a result half the network, some 150 people, were caught, among them Weidner's own sister, Gabrielle. She died in a concentration camp.

The so-called Palestine pioneers, the only resistance group with an outspoken Jewish character, were also active in finding escape routes: a Zionist training farm near the village of Loosdrecht served as the organisational centre. The most important organiser of the group, the non-Jew Joop Westerweel, dedicated himself to saving young Jewish boys who wanted to emigrate to Palestine. In close cooperation with a German Jewish refugee, Joachim Simon, nicknamed Schuschu, he organized the crossings over the Dutch border. Many of them were saved and did reach Palestine, but Schuschu was caught and shot himself. Joop Westerweel was also captured and executed in August 1944. During his custody in concentration camp Vught (near 's Hertogenbosch in the south of the Netherlands), he managed to write a last letter to his friends:

> You know that I won't betray anybody. I am positive about that. Committing suicide? I can do that the same way my good friend (Schuschu) did. I think of him a lot these days. Mentally I am still unbroken, at night I conquer the pain and the depressing feeling in my head in order to be fresh for the new interrogations in the morning. I want to carry on...Love to you all...Joop. (Bericht, 1971:1492, own translation)

Joop Westerweel died without having informed on his comrades.

*

In Amsterdam night after night, Dutch and German policemen were sent out with orders to round up the victims in their own homes. The majority of them were temporarily assembled in the *Hollandsche Schouwburg* (Dutch, later Jewish Theatre) on the edge of the Jewish neighbourhood.[8] From there, they were transported by tram and train to the transit camp of Westerbork. The atmosphere in the erstwhile theatre was one of nervous tension. Nobody knew exactly what to expect: men, women, children, Jewish Council officials, Dutch policemen, German guards, everybody was milling about.

Grete Weil, a Jewish refugee who had emigrated in the Thirties to Amsterdam, described her stay in the *Hollandsche Schouwburg* in *Ans Ende der Welt* (To the End of the World). She tells how the German commandant and Jewish Council officials sat for long hours, negotiating about the

In the beginning Jews were stil allowed to go out into the backyard of the Hollandsche Schouwburg to get some fresh air. Later that would also be forbidden

number of Jews who had to go on transport. It seemed to her as if they were talking about cattle, trading one off against the other:

"Seven of them have a Jewish Council stamp, and 15 have a Wehrmacht-'Sperre'." (...) "Does it really have to be 300? 275 should also be sufficient." "290." "Maybe only 280?" "285. But that's as far as I go." And that would be it. 285 would go on transport. But it was not numbers at all. These were men, women and children with dark, large, melancholy eyes, furriers and bankers, rag-and-bone men and scholars, diamond cutters and factory-owners. There were people that hated and people that loved... (Weil, 1989:74, own translation)

In the *Hollandsche Schouwburg* one of the first of many selections, eventually ending in the extermination camps, would take place. The drunken German commandant, who was on his way home, suddenly insisted he wanted to inspect the feet of the female prisoners:

On the first straw mattress near the door, an old working class woman looked at him drunk with sleep. "Pigs," he said loudly. "Sows. All Jews are pigs. Show me your filthy feet." The woman sat up straight and obediently pulled back the blanket. "I knew it," the Hauptsturmführer shouted, "the sow has filthy feet. She must also go on transport." He reeled a little and went to the next straw mattress with a young pretty woman on it. "Show me your feet." Quickly she got up and held her leg up. "Oh, oh, she has washed herself. Nice and clean you are. I like that. Get dressed and go home." The woman looked at him unbelievingly. Already a young boy from the Jewish Council had taken her by the hand and drawn her out of the bedroom. "Quickly," he whispered, "before he is sorry." (Weil, 1989:77, own translation)

With the help of resistance groups dedicated to getting the children out, a relatively large number of children – more than 1100 – was rescued from the *Schouwburg*. Because the *Schouwburg* was very overcrowded, many children were kept in the Kindergarten across the street. From there they were lifted over the wall to the adjoining Teacher's Training College. In rucksacks, potato sacks, laundry baskets or during a walk with prams, the babies and children were whisked to safety from under the noses of the Nazis. The resistance tried to find safe addresses and foster parents for them, which often proved more difficult and hazardous than getting them out of the Schouwburg. One of those children would later become Mayor of Amsterdam.

In spite of the courageous efforts of some, the Dutch resistance was too late in its response to the deportations to save a significant percentage of Jews from deportation. Only after the German defeat at Stalingrad in January 1943 were several effective resistance organisations developed. As the war dragged on and drained the available manpower, the German war machine needed more and more forced labour from other countries. In general, one may say that the Germans had fewer and fewer qualms about exploiting the occupied countries. This exploitation drove people to more militant opposition. The resistance movements in Holland developed through assisting people to hide from forced employment in Germany. They also spied on the Germans, committed sabotage, organized the underground press and began to prepare for liberation. All this, however, came too late to do anything effective for the Jews. In the underground papers very little was written about the deportations to the death camps.

From the beginning of 1943 onwards, the thorough Germans made no exception for Jewish hospitals and psychiatric institutions. It was difficult to believe that 'employment in the East' would benefit from hospitalised people, people from old-age homes, orphanages and mental homes. Dutch author Gerard Reve wrote a novella shortly after the war about how the family of the main character falls victim to the Nazis one by one, without even mentioning the word 'Jew'. It has been called a 'monument of silence'. In a sober, detached tone the decline of the family is described through the eyes of a young boy who initially looked upon the war as a welcome break from a stifling family existence:

"What I'd like best is short, violent street fighting here in town," I said. "From window to window, with handgrenades and white flags. But not for more than two days, because then it would be boring again." (Van het Reve, 1973:255)

Young and old, all would be 'employed' in 'labour' camps

First, his aunt and cousin were taken from their house at night – his incapacitated uncle Hans was in hospital at that time, and their mentally disturbed son Otto in the psychiatric hospital 'Het Apeldoornse Bos':

> Uncle Hans said nothing when he heard the news. They thought he hadn't heard or hadn't really understood, and they repeated it emphatically several times. He tried to raise himself up, and after they had put a pillow behind his back he sat looking out of the window. Finally, the visitors (...) went home again.
>
> One day some time later, a neighbour came to visit. "They are emptying the Invalide" (= De Joodsche Invalide: Jewish hospital in Amsterdam) she said. She had watched while hundreds of very old people were taken down the stairs and out of the building to vehicles standing ready for them. One 92-year-old man whom she thought she had known once had called out, "They're waiting on me hand and foot." "Het Apeldoornse Bos was emptied yesterday, too, " she said.
>
> "What did you say about Otto?" I asked my mother when she came back from her next visit to Uncle Hans.
>
> "The truth – that everything was taken away," she said. "He only hopes he's put to death right away. The doctors and nurses stayed with the patients, did you know that?" (Van het Reve, 1973:270)

'Het Apeldoornse Bos' was cleared by the Germans led by SS-Hauptsturmführer Aus der Fünten himself in the night of 21/22 January 1943, during which the most gruesome events took place. The whole medical staff and nurses chose voluntarily not to let their patients go alone and went along. One of the nurses was Claartje van Aals. She had a good address to go into hiding, but chose to stay. On the day of the evacuation, she wrote her last letter to her best friend:

> Today we will go. We don't know where yet, and we don't know either what will happen to the people. It is very chaotic. I am writing in the passage, and I am ridiculously calm (...) I have to leave everything behind, I can only take what is absolutely necessary. What will happen to us? I feel like I am drunk. If I wanted to, I could go into hiding, but I feel compelled to go with the people, because that's where the heart is(...) I must stop. (Wyers, 1995:106, own translation)

She never had time to finish the letter. All patients were thrown into lorries with great violence, taken to the station and from there in cattle trucks to Auschwitz. Thirteen hundred patients and 50 staff members were gassed immediately upon arrival.

*

Many Jews who wanted to escape 'the forced labour under police protection in Germany' tried to hide. But, as mentioned earlier, that was not easy, certainly not in the beginning. In the first place, one needed a great deal of money. In many cases it was not cheap to stay with non-Jews: they had to be trusted to buy food in large quantities (usually on the expensive black market), they sometimes charged high rents, they sometimes asked for hush money, allegedly to keep curious neighbours silent. Many considered going into hiding a greater danger than registering for transport. Despite their fear of treachery and of arrest by the SD (=Sicherheitsdienst/Security Police), 25,000 Jews, among them many children, did go into hiding in Holland. About 16,000 survived the war, so that one third, or about 8000, were eventually either detected or betrayed, as was the case with the Frank family. In no other Western European country did people go into hiding on such a large scale as in Holland.

The rescuers, on the other hand, also faced grave risks. They had to worry about getting food, which was becoming increasingly complicated: food was rationed through a coupon system. Later in the war there simply was not enough available. Miep Gies, who looked after the eight people hiding behind Otto Frank's office, tells how she had to visit an increasing number of shops to obtain a decreasing quantity of groceries. An even greater risk was death or disease in hiding. In *Anne Frank Remembered*, Miep Gies writes:

> By winter of 1943 it seemed as if all the Jews in Amsterdam were gone. Certainly just about all the Jews in South Amsterdam were no longer to be seen. Either they had been deported or they were in hiding or had somehow fled.(...) About

Jewish children in hiding on a Dutch farm: among many other new habits they had to learn to walk in clogs

the only time a Jew was seen now was floating face down in a canal. Sometimes they were thrown there by the very people who had hidden them, for one of the worst situations that could arise for us helpers was if someone in hiding died. What to do with the body? It was a terrible dilemma, as a Jew could not properly be buried. The second worst fear of people in hiding and for those who were hiding them was what to do if someone got sick? (Gies, 1987:131)

The case of the Frank family was a rather unusual one: very few Jews had a hiding place of their own like the one Anne's father constructed at the back of his office. Most were hidden in the homes of non-Jews. In some places only one Jew was given shelter, in others, mostly on the larger farms, ten or even more. In a provocative essay the psychologist Bruno Bettelheim has questioned the way Otto Frank had seen fit to provide for his family. He claims that to go into hiding together was a most silly thing to do, as *to hide out together made detection by the SS most likely; and when detected, everybody was doomed.* Bettelheim would have liked *each family member* [hiding] *with a different gentile family.* Likewise, he accuses Otto Frank of not planning a proper defence: *Had they had a gun, Mr. Frank could have shot down at least one or two of the 'green police' who came for them* and *even a butcher's knife, which they certainly could have taken with them into hiding, could have been used by them in self-defence.* (Bettelheim, 1979:248/249)

We feel that, however reasonable Bettelheim's charge at first sight might seem, he has not taken the reality of wartime Holland into account. It was difficult enough to find a Dutch family willing to take one Jew in, let alone to find eight families to shelter the eight people hiding in the 'Achterhuis.'[9] Also, the eight people were not detected by the SS, but betrayed by some unknown Dutchman. Taking into consideration that the eight managed to stay undetected for 25 months (July 1942 – August 1944), one can only conclude that their hiding place was not that easily detected. As far as the gun and the butcher's knife are concerned, one can only assume that these remarks are more inspired by the circumstances in Bettelheim's native Austria than by the reality of SS-occupied Holland. Equally unrealistic is his remark about the lack of an escape plan in case of discovery; a second exit would have brought the people in hiding only to a closed-off courtyard, from which there was no other way out than through another house.

It was not until the middle of 1943 that resistance organisations managed to find shelter for a considerable number of Jews, but by then the majority of them had already been deported. One of the main tasks of the Dutch resistance was the finding and organizing of hiding places. An estimated 3000 resistance workers were engaged in finding good hiding places, new identity papers, food coupons and money for Jews in hiding. In *Bitter Herbs* the main character is handed a new identity card:

> "What name have you given me?" I asked. "A beautiful one," he answered.(...) In the bus, I looked at the identity card. At my photograph with fair hair, and my thumbprint. I read the name. It was as if I was being introduced to myself. I murmured it under my breath a few times. I had become someone else. (Minco, 1960:109)

Proportionately, the Orthodox Protestants or Calvinists harboured more Jews than any other communal group, because many Calvinists regarded themselves as united to Jews by a bond of being two chosen people. Many times, resistance workers had to solve endless and often nerve-racking problems: boredom, arguments with the Christian environment, betrayal, (sexual) exploitation. In the novel *Kort Amerikaans* (American Crew Cut) by Jan Wolkers, a hidden Jewish girl is 'comforted' by her middle-aged host. In her defence she remarks to her friend:

> Try to understand. I have been alone for years. I can't go into the street, I don't see anyone. I am locked up here with those old people. It just happened, it was all I had. (Wolkers, 1962:164, own translation)

Moving to another address was a regular occurrence; it is estimated that most hidden Jews had to change their address at least three or four times for security reasons. The young Dutch writer Andreas Burnier even had to go into hiding at 16 different addresses. Apart from having to disguise her Jewishness, she also had trouble with her sexual identity: she felt like a boy

Members of the 'Help for the departing' committee of the Jewish Council stand behind their counter, certain of their 'Sperre'

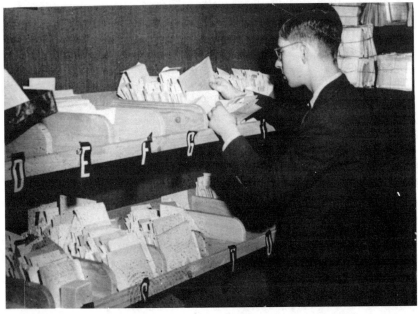

The Jewish Council organized a postal service between Holland and Auschwitz. They found that more letters were written from Holland, but that few came back. No action was taken

in the body of a girl, as we can read in her novel, *Het Jongensuur* (Boys' Hour).

According to De Jong, Jews in hiding were convinced that in most cases deportation would lead to their physical destruction. On the other hand, Jews who were deported believed they would manage in Poland.

*

The Jewish Council knew that the majority of Jews were deported to Auschwitz and the few letters received from there were comforting: hygiene was described as 'satisfactory', the general treatment as 'correct' and *there are magnificent shower arrangements with hot and cold water*. This supported the Council's view that the 'labour camps' in Upper Silesia (Poland) were nothing like the notorious Mauthausen concentration camp. All the rumors about systematic killings were therefore considered as horror propaganda. This passivity in Jewish circles in general led to an equally passive attitude among non-Jews. Non-involvement was the prevailing Dutch attitude. It is true that the churches (Protestant and Roman Catholic) protested in a telegram to Seyss-Inquart against the deportations as early as July 1942, a telegram which in the Catholic Churches and in a smaller Protestant denomination was read out from the pulpit. As a reprisal – and as a device to split the Churches – the Germans picked up and sent to the 'East' 700 Catholics of Jewish descent, among them the famous philosopher-nun Edith Stein, who died in Auschwitz.

What about the man in the street? Abel Herzberg writes about the big razzia of 20 June 1943, when 5,500 Jews were picked up at random. One of the assembly points was a square in Amsterdam with a large sports ground. It was a beautiful Sunday, and tennis matches were being played. The waiting Jews heard the sound of the balls and the calls of the players. Herzberg remarks:

> It was not NSB-men who were playing there. It was not men from the resistance. It was the majority of the Dutch people. They had got used to a lot. (Herzberg, 1985:154, own translation)

And Moshe Flinker, in Brussels, often wonders how people can still be happy while such terrible things are going on. After he had heard that a family known to him in hiding had been deported, he wrote:

> I don't know what to think, what to say, what to do. I see in the streets that the gentiles are happy and gay, and that nothing touches them. It is like being in a great hall where many people are joyful and dancing and also where there are a few people who are not happy and who are not dancing. And from time to time a few people of this latter kind are taken away, led to another room, and

Illegally taken photograph of Jews who are on their way to one of the assembly points in Amsterdam, 20 June 1943

strangled. The happy, dancing people in the hall do not feel this at all. Rather, it seems as if this adds to their joy and doubles their happiness. (Flinker, 1965:71)

Dance halls were full, cinema attendances were higher than ever, the beaches were as popular as always. Sports events in general, soccer in particular, drew large crowds to the stadiums. Were they not aware of the sufferings of the Jews? They were, but *there was nothing you could do about it* and *we had enough problems of our own.* Typical is the exclamation of one of the characters in S. de Vries' novel *Verduisterde jaren* (Darkened Years):

> Sometimes I don't know what to do with myself, because I am so mad that I sit here and do nothing. And what should I do, what can I do? I work in the chemist shop and when I am home, I am by myself. And the more I think about it, the more upset I become. Sometimes I think: You have believed in God so many years. You have gone to church, you have prayed and sung psalms. And now this has come and God allows it and sees it. Is that possible? Is this really possible? (De Vries, 1945:190, own translation)

Civil servants, policemen, railroad employees, everybody had a family to support: *the sense of responsibility towards the family was never greater than during the years of the occupation,* resistance fighter Henk van Randwijk noted sarcastically.

One of the endless registrations in Amsterdam, 20 May, 1943

Civil servants did their job: they stamped J's on identity documents, confiscated Jewish radios and Jewish bicycles, and sent unemployed Jews to labour camps. Never – even at the height of the razzias – were there more than 200 German policemen stationed in Amsterdam. The rest was done by Dutch policemen. In Harry Mulisch's successful novel *The Assault*, about a German act of reprisal after resistance fighters killed a collaborating police officer, there is a curious scene in a police station: German soldiers take young Anton Steenwijk, the only survivor of his family, to a police station, where he is to spend the night. The waiting room is full of Dutch policemen:

> A police sergeant carrying a grey horse blanket over his arm came over and told Anton to follow him. In the hall a second policeman joined them. He carried a bunch of keys in his hand. 'What do we have now?' he said when he saw Anton. 'Are we locking up children too? Or is he a little Jew?' 'Don't ask so many questions,' said the sergeant. (Mulisch, 1986:36)

It is characteristic of the half-protesting form of collaboration of most police officers that the second one wonders if they are incarcerating children as well now. *Or is he a little Jew?* he asks. Obviously, it would be a different matter then, a matter for the Germans only, not his responsibility.

A little further on in the same book, the son of the policeman killed by the resistance tries to defend the collaboration of his father. He says:

And all that stuff about the Jews; he didn't know a thing about that. He was ignorant of all that. You can't blame him for it, what the Germans did to them. He was with the police and simply did his duty, what he was told. Even before the war he had to arrest people, and he didn't know what would happen to them then, either. (Mulisch, 1986:102)

In other words, both events actually boil down to the same thing: before the war he had to arrest people, and during the war he had to arrest people. He was not responsible for what happened afterwards.

In Amsterdam and The Hague special units of fanatical Jew-hunters were formed within the police force to track down Jews. More Jews were caught by Dutch policemen than by Germans. The same phenomenon also occurred in occupied France and elsewhere. The financial reward for bringing in hidden Jews worked as a perverse incentive in these times of increasing scarcity. From the diary of one of these Jew-hunters:

Tonight Jew-hunt, very successful evening. I would think that I have caught at least a couple of hundred Jews in these past few weeks. Came home only at half past three this morning. A couple of days later he wrote: a comrade came to join in for a while and could return home with a full shopping-bag. (De Jong, 1966:380, own translation)

On the other hand, there were policemen who warned people in hiding when a razzia was imminent, just as there were civil servants who made forgeries of German *Ausweise* (identity documents) and other papers.

*

Between 15 July 1942 and 17 September 1944, the day of the last transport, 107,000 Jews were transported. The razzias continued all through the year, the trains left Westerbork every Tuesday morning. A total of 98 trains with more than a hundred thousand passengers could leave Holland without any incident. The involvement of Dutch authorities (civil servants, police, railway personnel) but also the cooperation of the Jewish Council, 'the State within a State'(Presser), contributed, according to Eichmann, to *such a smooth running of the transports that it was a pleasure to behold.*

Anne Frank

After the front door of Prinsengracht 263 closed behind Edith, Otto and
Anne Frank on Monday, 6 July 1942 – we walked in the pouring rain,
Daddy, Mummy, and I, each with a school satchel and shopping bag
filled to the brim with all kinds of things thrown together anyhow –
Margot had come earlier that same morning by bicycle with Miep
Gies. *None of them suspected it would not open to let them out again for
more than two years; and then it would only be under police escort following
their arrest. The events of those two years, the petty bickering between the
eight people in the hiding place, the rumors about the war outside, the
troubles the people in the front offices had to get them enough food, the little
flirtations – it has all been meticulously written down by Anne in her diary.
The shelter itself can only be called comfortable in comparison with the kind
of accommodation other Jews sometimes had to put up with in their efforts
to escape from the Nazis. Even after the Franks had been joined by the Van
Pels family – Herman and Augusta van Pels and their son Peter [10] – one
week later and by the dentist Dr Fritz Pfeffer in November 1942, it was still
manageable:* No one would ever guess that there were so many rooms
hidden behind that plain grey door, *Anne writes. This is not saying it
would have been easy to spend every day behind closed doors and blacked-out
windows, wary of every unexplained sound, careful not to make any noise,
bored and annoyed. It is to the credit of Otto Frank that he had realized at
an early stage that boredom would be their biggest enemy. He was a man of
foresight, as is borne out by his leaving Germany in 1933, by the aryanisa-
tion of his firm Opekta before it became enforced by decree, and by making
the preparations to go into hiding from about July 1941 onwards. He even
filed for emigration to the USA in 1940, but events caught up with him
before he could make his move. He decided the only way to combat the
inevitable boredom would be to have a rigid schedule every day that everybody would have to adhere to. The sea of time had to be structured in order
to avoid chaos and unbearable tensions. That explains the strict study
discipline he set his two daughters and Peter: every day, they would do
mathematics, German, English and stenography, there were fixed reading
hours, etc. It also explains the lengthy entries in Annes diary, the imaginary
letters she wrote to friends, the short stories she became quite good at. It is
interesting to see her development as a writer: how she grew from the shy
girl of 20 June 1942, who writes that she cannot imagine that anybody will
be interested in the unbosomings of a 13-year-old schoolgirl, to her trium-
phant entries of 4 April 1944:* I know that I can write, a couple of my
stories are good, my descriptions of the Secret Annexe are humorous,

there's a lot in my diary that speaks, but whether I have real talent remains to be seen, *and 11 May 1944:* My greatest wish is to become a journalist some day and later on a famous writer (...) I want to publish a book entitled *Het Achterhuis* after the war.

News from the world outside came to the people inside via two channels: from the helpers in the front office and from the radio in Otto Frank's office. Miep Gies, in particular, was bombarded with questions every day, when she came up to find out if there was anything in particular she had to try and buy. Food was rationed, the black market expensive and dangerous, commodities were getting scarcer all the time, but the people in the front office did what they could to buy what was necessary. So we find Anne Frank reporting from time to time about what is going on; we learn that Otto Frank has put up a map of Europe on the wall where he records the progress of the Allied armies with little pins.

From the diary we get an impression of what it is like when eight people are forced to spend every minute of the day together. On the other hand, all eight are constantly aware of how fortunate they are in comparison with what was going on outside. Anne Frank writes on 19 November 1942, for instance: Countless friends and acquaintances have gone to a terrible fate. Evening after evening the green and grey army lorries trundle past (...) I feel wicked sleeping in a warm bed, while my dearest friends have been knocked down; and on 13 January 1943, she writes: Day and night more of those poor miserable people are being dragged off, with nothing but a rucksack and a little money. (...) Families are torn apart, the men, women and children all being separated. And as for us, we are fortunate. Yes, we are luckier than millions of people.

On 4 August 1944 – a Friday – that luck ran out. That day, two months after the Allied landings in Normandy, some time between eleven and twelve in the morning, the house was raided by the police, after an anonymous tip-off. All eight people were arrested[11], so were two of the helpers of the office. The arresting policeman, an SD officer from Vienna called Karl Silberbauer[12], had them taken to the SD headquarters in the Euterpestraat in the south of Amsterdam. From there, they were brought to the House of Detention at the Weteringschans. On 8 August 1944 a train took them to Westerbork.

IV
The Transit Camps

I can see a father, ready to depart, blessing his wife and child and being himself blessed in turn by an old rabbi with a snow-white beard and the profile of a fiery prophet. I can see...ah, I can't begin to describe it all... (Etty Hillesum)

All roads lead through Westerbork
(SS-Hauptsturmführer Aus der Fünten)

Ironically enough, *Polizeiliches Durchgangslager Westerbork* (Police Transit Camp Westerbork) began its short unhappy life as a Dutch project. In February 1939 the Dutch Cabinet had decided to build a camp to house Jewish refugees from Germany. For the last lot of the more than 30,000 German and Austrian Jews who had entered Holland in the Thirties, it was difficult to find a place, not in the least because these latecomers were on the whole not as wealthy as those who had come between 1933 and 1937. This had led to enormous financial and accommodation problems. They became the charge of the Jewish Committee for Special Jewish Interests, private institutions and church organisations. The government wanted to make a camp available to them and put forward the money, on loan. Eventually, all of it would have to be repaid by the Jewish community. The chosen site – on the heathland of Drente – was in one of Holland's more desolate areas: bleak and wet in winter, sandy, dusty and full of flies in summer. One of the first refugees to enter the new site remembers:

> The further we walked, the more lonely it became. It was just heathland as far as the eye could see. An occasional shrub. Where the refugee camp was to be built, we saw a large plain of heath and sand, very desolate. But we had no say in the matter and had to be satisfied. (Quoted in Mulder, 1991:4, own translation)

That was 1939; in the winter of 1940, things had not improved much. Fred Schwarz, an Austrian immigrant from Vienna, was one of the first inhabitants of the new camp. He writes:

> I have no idea what the 'civilised' world looks like at the moment, but here it is a nightmare. Snowstorms are raging round the barracks, icicles are hanging from the leaking gutters. The heater in our washroom has given up, and therefore washing facilities and toilets are frozen. (Schwarz, 1994:87, own translation)

It had not been the government's first choice. That had been a site near Elspeet, nearer the centre of the country. One of the protests against this site had come from Queen Wilhelmina, who considered it too close to her private residence.

In October 1939 the first refugees arrived, all German Jews. That would become an important factor later: from 1942 Westerbork would be the central transit camp for all the Jews in Holland, and by then the German Jews had developed into some kind of camp aristocracy, the *alte Kamp Einsassen* (old camp inhabitants).

Westerbork would become the gateway to the camps in Poland, and consequently, the gateway to death for more than 100,000 Dutch Jews. *All roads lead through Westerbork*, SS-Hauptsturmführer Aus der Fünten once remarked to some Jews who had come to plead a postponement of deportation.

In July 1942 the German administration took over command of the camp. A high barbed-wire fence – later electrified – was put up, observation towers were built at intervals of every 200 meters, and these were manned by SS men, armed with machine guns. The camp administration was nominally the responsibility of the SS, but there was a strange twist. In advance of the arrival of the SS, the inhabitants of the camp had organised their own 'management' of the camp. Its aim was to serve as a 'buffer' between the Jews and the Germans, not unlike the way the leaders of the Jewish Council in Amsterdam thought about their council. As a result, the Germans were offered a ready-made administration which might otherwise have cost a lot of effort and manpower. So, apart from the armed SS members in the guard towers and a relatively small number in the camp itself, much of the actual administration was done by the Jews themselves. In other words, Jews were guarding Jews: Jews were barrack leaders, leaders of the labour commands, members of the Order Police (= OD), administrators, etc. In the end Jews were putting other Jews on transport: a form of collaboration that resulted in an ever decreasing number of Jews helping to deport an ever increasing number of other Jews. All with only one motive: to have an opportunity to avoid 'going on transport' for another couple of weeks, for one week maybe. A job meant a *Sperre*, also for one's direct family. A consequence of this arrangement was that most of the administrative jobs were in the hands of the 'old camp inhabitants'. The German Jews were there when the Germans took over in July 1942, and the latter saw no reason why they should change people they got on with, whom they could understand, and who did the job well. The Dutch Jews in the camp, however, became increasingly resentful of the German Jews; they accused them of being worse than the Germans themselves in order to ingratiate themselves with their masters. The epithet *Jewish SS* for the Order Police speaks volumes:

> Some of the OD men, Germans and Dutchmen, have been recruited from the dregs of Jewish society, rough, coarse fellows, without refinement, human feelings or compassion; they just live for their cigarettes and for an easy affair with women like themselves. Like the 'Green Police' (German Policemen), they

wear green uniforms and high jackboots. They base their uncouth behaviour on that of their German colleagues who are lavish in the use of their fists and inflict quick, hard punishment with their boots. The Jews in the camp refer to them as the Jewish SS. They are hated like the plague, and people would flay many of them alive if they dared. (Mechanicus, 1968:26)

Work in Westerbork consisted chiefly of camp maintenance and fatigue duties. Working hours were long, but most dreaded were the roll calls. As a rule there were three roll calls a day. People had to fall in line – amidst much screaming and shouting – in the large courtyard of the camp, and numbers were counted. This could take hours, especially if figures did not match, which frequently occurred. Both the sick and the dead were included in the roll call. It was frequently used as a form of punishment, when people had to stand at attention for hours in the cold and rain. If one of them collapsed, assistance was not allowed, and he/she had to be left until after the roll call.

*

Apart from writing history, Jacques Presser also tried his hand at writing novels and short stories. One of these, *De nacht der Girondijnen* (The Night of the Girondists), was published in 1957 and dealt with Westerbork. Presser put himself in the shoes of one of these hated OD men, Jewish collaborators of the worst kind. His main character is a history teacher who has become the deputy of Westerbork's Jewish second-in-command. The motto that precedes the text is *Homo Homini Homo*, man is to his fellow human beings not like the wolf (lupus) Hobbes thought him to be, but a man, a thousand times worse than the wolf. Where the wolf kills only for food, man kills for power, for politics, for pleasure, for nothing. He betrays his loved ones and is loyal to the one he hates. This is an apt description of the people called the Jewish SS. Presser describes one of the least palatable jobs of the OD: the reading of the list of people who were going to be transported the next day:

> The list was alphabetical, but nobody quite depended on it; only when I was finished did bedlam break out. I have seen people dancing, wild with joy, (...) kissing and laying hands upon one another in the most obscene fashion; others I have seen running as if they had taken leave of their senses, falling down and getting up again, over and over (...); I have seen a woman bite the jugular vein of her sister, whose name was not called, and who had thus escaped; and a man who put out his eyes right in front of me because another, three steps from me, was sitting sobbing with joy. I have seen it, seen it myself, many nights of perdition. I HAVE SEEN IT. (Presser, 1992:65)

Based on the observations by Mechanicus and Presser, one could easily conclude that there were very few feelings of solidarity between German

Jews and Dutch Jews. Be that as it may, Abel Herzberg is of a somewhat different opinion: in the diary that he kept in Bergen-Belsen, called *Twee-stroomenland* (Land of Two Streams), he has another explanation for the feelings of animosity between the Dutch and the Germans. He sees the need to distance oneself from anything German as the root of this lack of solidarity:

> They (the Dutch Jews) want to exhibit what good Dutchmen they are. Therefore, they have to distance themselves from any form of Jewish solidarity. (...) Of course, they speak a different language, so there is a linguistic difference, but any other difference is largely artificial. In general, Dutch Jews and German Jews are very much alike (...) The characteristics, usually ascribed to the German Jews, are for the larger part not characteristics at all, but good or bad habits that Dutch Jews have as well. The difference lies with the inclination to condone these habits or not. Everybody might have seen that there were Dutch Jews who easily adopted SS manners, as if they had never seen anything different. As soon as a German Jew took over these manners, anti-German feelings (...) were given free range. (Herzberg, 1950:78/79; own translation)

As a result of the very effective management of the camp, efforts to escape were few. It was considered an act of disloyalty towards one's fellow Jews, who were doing their best to make things as bearable as possible. The Germans from their side did everything to encourage this attitude and as a rule put ten extra people on transport for every escape attempt (only on one occasion were 50 extra people put on the train in reprisal for an unsuccessful attempt by a 12-year-old boy – see Etty Hillesum below).

We are relatively well-informed about life in the 'Jewish capital of Holland'. A number of diaries that were kept there have survived. In particular, the diaries of Etty Hillesum and Philip Mechanicus are important sources of information. In addition, there is the film *Westerbork*, made at the initiative of the camp commandant, SS-Obersturmführer Konrad Gemmeker. He was so proud of the smooth running of the camp under his command that he ordered a film to be made of it. It is not a propaganda film in the usual sense of the word, unlike the Nazi films of other camps – Theresienstadt and Auschwitz come to mind – and he did not ask for approval from either The Hague or Berlin. When he was asked at his trial in 1949 about the reasons for making this film, he answered:

> With this film, which was made for the camp and for showing in the camp, I tried to record everything, including the sadder aspects, in order that it might not be said that I only focused on the better side of the camp. (quoted in Boas, 1985:31)

The 'sadder aspects' are the scenes the whole world has become familiar with since then: they are included in almost every documentary on the Holocaust. The scenes on the platform of Jews boarding the train, the SS

Departure from Westerbork. The little push cart demonstrates the need for 'labour in the East'

officers standing around and smoking, their German shepherd dogs on a chain, the little girl looking out just before the door is closed, the train pulling away from the platform, the note that is thrown out of the speeding train. Because no matter how almost idyllic life in Westerbork might seem in the rest of the film – with its schools, its hospital, its theatre – these are the moments that no amount of editing can whitewash. This is where Westerbork showed its true face: deporting Jews to their deaths in Poland. Did people know what was waiting for them there? They could only suspect something sinister was happening. People cannot believe in their own death, while they are still young and strong. It is told by many that even those about to enter the gas chambers did not believe they would no longer be there in 15 minutes. But they were frightened. For that fear, deportation from Westerbork was the beginning. That is why Abel Herzberg wrote:

> Westerbork was another word for purgatory. There was nothing to sustain one, materially or spiritually. Each was thrown on his own resources, utterly alone. Desperation, total and absolute, seized everyone. People sought help but seldom found it and, if they did, knew that it could not possibly prevail. Deportation to Poland might at best be postponed – for a week, perhaps, or for a few weeks at most. Husbands were powerless to protect their wives, parents had to watch helplessly while their children were torn away from them for ever. The sick, the blind, the hurt, the mentally disturbed, pregnant women, the dying, orphans,

Children playing between the barracks of Westerbork

new-born babies – none was spared on the Tuesdays when the cattle-trucks were being loaded with human freight for Poland. Tuesdays, week in, week out, for two interminable years. (Abel Herzberg, cited in Presser, 1969:406)

It is impossible to do justice to the many paradoxes in this camp. The most striking one is the excellent medical care that people enjoyed. The people who would be put to death a couple of hundred miles to the east could here count on: a hospital with 1725 beds, 120 doctors and specialists, more than 1000 other staff, fully equipped labs, an outstanding pharmacy, clinics for outpatients, X-ray facilities, dental surgery, etc. Small wonder nobody believed the pessimists who were claiming it was all a farce and a façade. Who could understand a system that did its utmost to keep people alive in Holland, only to murder them a week or a few weeks later in Poland? The same can be said about the schools, the cabaret-revues, the classical concerts, the soccer and boxing matches. All these contributed to an eerie sense of normalcy and safety. The physician Elie Cohen, who had come to Westerbork after he had spent some time in punishment camp Amersfoort, wrote in *De afgrond* (The Abyss):

> Westerbork. It was sociable. We visited each other, we made appointments. There was whoring, there was flirting, there was drinking. Everything happened, just like in ordinary life. Only once every week there was that crazy train, which was to take a number of Jews away. Every list platzte some time or another, and one accepted that. But that it made one depressed for a long time, that is not true either. Not as far as I was concerned. Because ordinary life took over again afterwards. (Cohen, 1971:53; own translation)

As stated, the descriptions of camplife by Etty Hillesum and Philip Mechanicus make this microcosm and its inhabitants stand out in a stark and unforgiving light. It is like stepping through a mirror: nothing is any longer what it seems.

*

Etty Hillesum came from a learned and cultured family background. Her grandfather had been chief rabbi of the three Northern provinces of Holland, her father was a classical scholar and rector of a grammar school in Deventer. Etty (Esther) herself studied law, philosophy and languages in Amsterdam; her brother Mischa was one of Holland's most promising young pianists, her other brother Jaap was a doctor.

As a member (for a few weeks) of the Jewish Council, she seemed to have been able to travel up and down between Amsterdam and Westerbork quite frequently. She hated that job and herself for having applied for it. On 14 July 1942, she writes in her diary that she feels as if she had done something improper:

> Like crowding onto a small piece of wood adrift on an endless ocean after a shipwreck and then saving oneself by pushing others into the water and watching them drown. It is all so ugly.(...) I would much rather join those who prefer

to float on their backs for a while, drifting on the ocean with their eyes turned towards heaven and who then go down with a prayer. (Hillesum, 1983:152)

A similar sentiment is expressed by the young boy Moshe Flinker, who is for the moment safe in Brussels. He feels guilty about being safe, while 'his brothers' are being deported. He writes: *I, too, wish to suffer with my brothers, with my people, whom I love so much. My people, my people!* (Boas, 1995:99) Far from feeling that he had been saved to be a hope for *the future of my people*, he convinces himself that he is like a traitor *who fled from his people at the time of their anguish*. This feeling became so powerful at times that he considered volunteering for work in one of the labour camps:

> Often have I felt this yearning and need to be with them and participate in their sufferings (...) I should go to the Germans and say that I wish to go and work, then they would doubtlessly take me. But at least for the time being, I am sure that my father would not let me do any such thing. (Boas, 1995:100)

After a while, Etty Hillesum began to look upon life in Amsterdam – with its frantic search for good hiding-places and exemptions from transport (*Sperre*) – as even more artificial than life in the camp. It was not as if she had any illusions about the ultimate aim of the Nazis; earlier than most, she realised what the Nazis had in store for the Jews. On 3 July 1942 – almost two weeks before the first transport from Westerbork to Auschwitz – she writes about her 'new certainty'. That certainty is that the Nazis are after 'our total destruction'. She decides, however, not to burden others with her fears. She continues in her diary:

> I shall not be bitter if others fail to grasp what is happening to us Jews. I work and continue to live with the same conviction, and I find life meaningful – yes, meaningful – although I hardly dare say so in company these days. (Hillesum, 1983:130)

In Westerbork she found her calling. She developed into a radiant woman, dispensing comfort, kind words and concrete help. She became what she wanted to be: *be willing to act as a balm for all wounds* (last words of the part of her diary that survived, Saturday, 10 October 1943). In between she found time to write and send long letters to her friends. In them, she gives her impressions of the netherworld she was inhabiting. She writes: *The misery here is really indescribable*. But she made herself go on. On 10 July 1943 she writes:

> You know, if you don't have the inner strength while you're here to understand that all outer appearances are a passing show, as nothing beside the great splendour (I can't think of a better word right now) inside us – then things can look very black here indeed. Completely wretched, in fact, as they must look to those pathetic people who have lost their last towel, who struggle with boxes,

trays of food, cups, mouldy bread and dirty laundry, on, under and around their bunks, who are miserable when other people shout at them or are unkind, but who shout at others without a thought; or to those poor abandoned children whose parents have been sent on transport, and who are ignored by the other mothers: they have worries enough with their own brood, what with the diarrhoea and all the other complaints, big and small, when nothing was ever wrong with them in the past. You should see these poor mothers sitting beside the cots of their wailing young in blank and brute despair. (Hillesum, 1983:203)

On her rounds through the hospital wards, she came across the strangest of scenes: a 9-month-old baby with a 'criminal record', because of having been abandoned by her parents, which made her an S-case (S for *straf* = punishment); a mother saying to her children: 'if you don't eat up straight-away, mummy won't be coming on the transport with you.' But the saddest story comes in her long letter of 24 August 1943. In it, she describes the night before a transport, the hellish night from Monday to Tuesday. Although she confesses: *I have told you often enough that no words and images are adequate to describe nights like these*, she continues to say that she feels she has a duty: *One always has the feeling here of being the ears and eyes of a piece of Jewish history.* Eventually, she recounts the story that contains the essence of life in the camps, all the cruelty, bad luck, viciousness and arbitrariness of it. It is the story of a young boy:

He had thought he was safe, that was his mistake, and when he realised he was going to have to go anyway, he panicked and ran off. His fellow Jews had to hunt him down – if they didn't find him, scores of others would be put on the transport in his place. He was caught soon enough, hiding in a tent, but 'notwithstanding'...'notwithstanding', all those others had to go on transport anyway, as a deterrent, they said. And so, many good friends were dragged away by that boy. Fifty victims for one moment of insanity. Or rather: he didn't drag them away – our commandant did, someone of whom it is sometimes said that he is a gentleman. Even so, will the boy be able to live with himself, once it dawns on him exactly what he's been the cause of? And how will all the other Jews on board the train react to him? That boy is going to have a very hard time. (Hillesum, 1983:208)

What, she wonders, would she be saying if she wrote that she was living in hell that night? Once the train has moved out, she says:

We know nothing of their fate. It is only a short while, perhaps, before we find out, each one of us in his own time, for we are all marked down to share that fate, of that I have not a moment's doubt. (Hillesum, 1983:219)

Two weeks later she would find out: together with her parents and her brother Misha she was transported to Auschwitz-Birkenau (*I have my diaries, my little Bible, my Russian grammar and Tolstoy with me and God knows what else,* she said to a friend). She died in Auschwitz on 30 November 1943.

*

A comparison of the diaries of Etty Hillesum and Philip Mechanicus illustrates a kind of analysis of what Jacques Presser called 'ego-documents': a category of memories that diaries share with published memoirs and correspondences, a category therefore in which a subject is very much present. Presser further refines this for diaries and discerns *external* from *intimate* diaries. In the first category, that of external diaries, the author observes and notes down events and other people's responses to them; in the intimate diary the author's concern is to record his/her own impressions and reflections.

If we adopt that difference between external and intimate diaries for the purpose of this book, it is clear that Etty Hillesum's diary falls into the latter category, whereas Mechanicus' obviously belongs in the first. This is not to say that personal reflections are completely absent in *Waiting for Death*, nor that Hillesum does not describe events, but the emphasis is clearly different. That is not to be wondered at: Mechanicus was a professional journalist, a reporter with one of Holland's leading newspapers. Reporting must have come naturally to him. In Westerbork he observed and reported on the mood in the camp, on the monotony[1], on the tensions between the different groups, the cabaret shows, the schools, the love affairs, the orphanage, the lack of privacy, the rumors, camp humour and camp language, the personalities of Gemmeker and of Kurt Schlesinger, his Jewish second-in-command ('the powerless Potentate', as Presser called him), and inevitably the train. The train that divides the week – before Tuesday morning 11 a.m. and after – the train that divides the camp, the train that divides people.

> The transports are as loathsome as ever. The wagons used were originally intended for carrying horses. The deportees no longer lie on straw, but on the bare floor in the midst of their food supplies and small baggage, and this applies even to the invalids who only last week got a mattress. They are assembled at the hut exits at about seven o'clock by OD men, the men of the Camp Security Police, and are taken to the train in lines of three, to the Boulevard des Misères in the middle of the camp. The train is like a long mangy snake, dividing the camp in two and made up of filthy old wagons. The Boulevard is a desolate spot, barred by OD men to keep away interested members of the public. (Mechanicus, 1968:25)

Did they know what was waiting for them in Poland? They did not know anything for certain, but they knew something sinister was threatening. Mechanicus mentions several cases of suicide:

Early this morning two men in my hut tried to commit suicide. Unsuccessfully. One of them cut his jugular vein and the knife was wrenched out of the hand of the other man before he could harm himself. The house physician did an excellent job. A mood of depression and great emotion. (Mechanicus, 1968:68)

But most people did not anticipate death, even those about to enter the gas chambers. One suppresses the thought of the worst and prefers to believe any deception.

By Nazi standards Westerbork was a 'humane' camp. In the camp musical 'revues' were performed with an elite of Dutch and German artists. Mechanicus wrote about *operetta music at an open grave*, not completely without reason when we realise that the weekly revue was performed on a Tuesday evening, the evening after the train had left in the morning. The idea behind it was to take people's minds off that subject. Shows were held in the same barrack 9 – partly built from wood broken out of the synagogue in Assen – that was by day the registration hall. Women behind typewriters and men with long questionnaires were replaced by an audience only too willing to have a good time. We had *the best cabaret in Europe*, one of the artistes, Jetty Cantor, would say after the war. Six large revues were performed between 1942 and 1944, all written and directed by Max Ehrlich, Willy Rosen and Erich Ziegler, famous names from the Roaring Twenties in Berlin. Another attraction were *Johnny and Jones, two boys with a guitar*, who had been very popular in Amsterdam. They sang jazzy songs in Dutch with a mock American accent. Camp commandant Gemmeker encouraged the shows as much as he could, using among other means, the exemption of the artistes from transport (*bis auf weiteres* – until further notice – of course; because in the end all of them ended up either in Theresienstadt or in Auschwitz).

Etty Hillesum writes about Gemmeker and his love for the arts:

He could be said to be our artistic patron here, and is a regular at all our cabaret nights. On one occasion he came three times in succession to see the same performance and roared with laughter at the same old jokes each time. Under his auspices, a male choir has been formed that sang 'Bei mir bist du schön' on his personal orders. It sounded very moving here on the heath, it must be said. (Hillesum, 1983, 217)

Mechanicus is also of two minds about the cabarets; he seems to have had fewer reservations about the soccer matches and the performances of the symphony orchestra. In the latter, half of the pre-war members of the Amsterdam Concertgebouw Orchestra were playing. Humor, no matter how mild, however, he found debatable under the circumstances in which the prisoners were living. He observes a sharp difference in the reactions of the audience, depending on age. On 16 September 1943, he notes:

Went to see the revue once again yesterday evening. Packed out.(...)The response of the audience is mixed. There is great admiration for the work of the cast, and people laugh at the jokes and enjoy the words and the music about the camp and the comments of the entertainer(...) But the majority of the audience are not at all willing to let themselves go – they seem inhibited. The invitation (...) to join in and sing the catchy choruses altogether gets a response only from some of the young people. The older generation keep quiet and cannot relax after all the suffering they have gone through and are still going through daily. Also in the matter of applause the older generation are restrained, but the younger generation are open-hearted and burst out from time to time into rhythmical handclapping.(...) Over this whole revue an atmosphere of painful melancholy and suffering hangs like a haze. (Mechanicus, 1968:159)

In September 1944 – the Allied Armies had already liberated the south of Holland – all artistes were deported. Most of them were first taken to Theresienstadt where some of them were involved in the making of the film *Der Führer schenkt die Juden eine Stadt* (The Führer Gives a City to the Jews). Afterwards, they were taken to Auschwitz together with all the extras and murdered there. Others came directly to Auschwitz, and when that camp was evacuated, they were spread over a number of other camps. Very few of them survived the war.

Vught

At the beginning of 1943, another concentration camp in Holland, Vught, near the southern town of 's Hertogenbosch, became a police transit camp, like Westerbork. The Germans wanted to have all Jews behind barbed wire, even if they could not be deported to Poland immediately. They believed that the remaining Jews would be a source of unrest and possible resistance. Westerbork was considered too small and therefore another camp had to be built. The first half-year was bad: food was scarce, virtually no medical care, health conditions appalling. Three hundred and eleven prisoners died, 170 in the first six weeks. After protests from outside, life improved. In Westerbork, which was much better organised, death was relatively rare. It seemed at one stage as if Vught would develop into a 'normal' concentration camp and not into a transit camp. Leaders from the Jewish Council heard that Jews would be put to work. If you go to Vught, you don't go to Poland, people told one another.

Days were long: the prisoners were woken up at about 4 a.m. (4:45 in winter) and went to bed at 9.30 p.m. They had a 12-hour working day, in the beginning spent on the construction of the camp (building of barracks, laying out of roads), but from the spring of 1943 a branch of the Philips factory in Eindhoven was brought to the camp and provided hundreds of inmates with (very cheap) work on radios, small dynamos, etc. The work on the radios made it possible to listen to secret broadcasts on the progress of the war, with the unique result that these prisoners were very well-informed people.[2] They passed on their news to others in the camp. This listening to 'illegal' news on the BBC was punished severely when detected. The favourite punishment was 'flogging': the victim was stripped down to the waist, he had to lie down on a block, was held by OD men, and between ten to fifty strokes were administered with a stick on his bare back. All this took place in the courtyard in full view of everybody. Other offences that would invite floggings included smoking when prohibited, wearing two layers of underclothes, offending a guard by not greeting him respectfully, stealing from the kitchen, talking about the war, etc. In Vught and other camps there were dogs specially trained to attack the inmates. Apart from flogging, the most frequent 'punishment' was having to lie down in the mud, crawl through it, stand up, lie down again, and so on, ad infinitum. It was in Vught that one of the most serious tragedies in the history of the camps in Holland occurred, an event that has become known as 'the bunker drama': 91 women were locked up in two small cells and left without food and water, without light and air. In the standing room only, women began to faint, scream and curse. After 17 hours ten women had died, a number had gone insane, many more were unconscious. The corpses were cremated in great secrecy.

The expectation of the Jews in Vught that they would stay in Holland proved untrue. In June 1943, thousands of people, including 1200 children under 16 were, suddenly ordered to leave the camp. People reacted to this announcement *with a roar I am not likely to hear again*, writes history student David Koker in his diary. Old men and women, mothers with nursing babies in their arms, some wrapped in blankets and others exposed, howling little girls and others unconscious of what was happening, men and women with sacks, trunks, pails, pans and bottles; sick and healthy, old and young, children without parents, whole families together – all were first taken to Westerbork and from there to Sobibor. They were all killed on arrival.

No matter how heartbreaking Koker thought these deportations were, it is characteristic of him that he never ceases to try and understand the Germans:

All the inconsistencies here are dogmas that collide, but do not exclude one another. Collectively and individually the German wants to do everything perfectly. Collectively, they want to give the Jews as good a treatment as possible, although they consider them their mortal enemy. Of course within their own rigorous ways and according to their norms, but still, within that framework perfectly. Individually, they even feel something for those people, even though they only show this on rare occasions, like with this children transport. (Koker, 1977: 132, own translation)

The Germans even had flowerbeds with geraniums laid out. Koker comments:

> But again oversystematised, just as the pleasure of the cabaret revue was killed completely by the (...) pompous entourage. In a way, I would say, the Germans want us to be happy here. Not out of friendliness, I should think, but out of that tendency for completeness that possesses them in everything. (Koker, 1977: 132, own translation)

Vught was not a camp far removed from the 'normal' world. Prisoners did not feel they inhabited another planet, as in Westerbork. Yet they might as well have, seeing the way the people in the village turned their heads when they saw the prisoners coming past. Koker writes about this alienation between victims and bystanders:

> I almost had tears in my eyes when I went through the village and saw all the living rooms. How far away we were already! And those people on their way home. Many holiday-makers putting on a pious face when we go by, with our yellow stars and our SS man behind us. (Koker, 1977:123, own translation)

Like many diarists Koker found distraction and elevation in reading and studying. He also wrote poetry. David Koker wrote his last occasional poem for a little girl in Vught on New Year's Eve, 1944. A year later he died during a transport of the sick from Gross-Rosen to Dachau:

A somber fate awaits us:

Boredom to the bitter end,
When the last man vanishes
Like a dirty cloud of smoke through the chimney.

My poems disappear like smoke,
Yet I put them together
Though I don't know if you'll ever hear
A little song of the bitter end.

The smoke blows away and leaves no trace.
I cannot remain upright any longer.
It is better to leave early
Like a cloud of smoke through the chimney,
Than all those years of boredom
And still the same bitter end.
(Koker, 1977:21, own translation)

Anne Frank

After their arrest and their subsequent imprisonment in the House of Detention Weteringschans, the Franks, the Van Pelses and Fritz Pfeffer were transported to Westerbork as so-called punishment cases on 8 August 1944. Their crime had been not reporting for deportation, and trying to evade it by going into hiding. Punishment cases did not qualify for any 'Sperre' and were usually deported on the next train to the east. Not much is known about their stay in Westerbork. In Willy Lindwer's compilation of interviews with women who knew Anne Frank in the last seven months of her life, Rachel van Amerongen-Frankfoorder tells the story of how she was approached by Otto Frank. He asked her if Anne could work with her in the internal service of Westerbork: scrubbing, cleaning the toilets, handing out overalls, etc. She says: She was really so sweet, a little older than she was in the photo that we've all seen, gay and cheerful. Unfortunately, I had no say in the matter. *(Lindwer, 1991:92). In the interview with Janny Brandes-Brilleslijper, we read that Anne Frank worked at the batteries, like most women:* That was very messy work, and no one could understand the reason for it. We had to chop open the batteries with a chisel and a hammer and then throw the tar in one basket and the carbon bars, which we had to remove, into another basket; we had to take off the metal caps with a screwdriver, and they went into a third basket. In addition to getting terribly dirty from the work, we all began to cough because it gave off a certain kind of dust. The agreeable part of working on the batteries was that you could talk with each other...The Frank girls were there. We sat at long tables while we split the batteries. *(Lindwer, 1991:52)*

From other reports Anne seems to have enjoyed being in Westerbork: after having been locked up inside for more than two years, she probably liked the sun and the opportunity to walk and talk with other people. People felt confident that as the war was nearing its final stages – the Allied Armies were in Paris by now and nearing the border of the south of Holland – they would not be leaving Holland. They would survive the war in Westerbork. But then there came news that there was to be one last final transport. Pandemonium broke out, a desperate struggle not to be on that transport list. Everyone tried to pull all the strings they had, but the people in the punishment barrack had no illusions. They were certain of transport. When the list was read out on Monday evening, 2 September, all eight people from Prinsengracht 263 were on it. On 3 September the very last train to leave Westerbork for Auschwitz[3] left the makeshift station of the transit camp: on board were 498 men, 442 women, 79 children – a total of 1019 people.

V
The Railroad of No Return

The world has changed. (David Koker, November 27, 1943)

This is a page of glory in our history, which has never been written and is never to be written. (Speech of Heinrich Himmler, October 14, 1943)

Probably during the late summer of 1941, the decision to exterminate all the Jews in occupied Europe had been taken, and this was followed by the coordination of the enterprise at Wannsee in January 1942. From then on, trains ran day and night to the extermination centres in Poland.

David Koker heard the word extermination for the first time in transit camp Vught, in the beginning of September 1943. He was at that time still reasonably optimistic, an optimism that would soon vanish. On 27 November a letter from Poland took his last doubts away, when he read that most of the Jews were murdered on arrival. *The world has changed*, was his only comment. (Koker, 1977:201)

In general, Koker proved well-informed; for instance, he knew that 'special cases' went to 'different camps', *all the rest just go to Auschwitz*. He was right. The large majority of Jews from Holland were transported to Auschwitz, the rest went to Sobibor and only a few thousands to Theresienstadt and Bergen-Belsen.[1]

All witnesses of those train journeys to Poland speak of the same kind of frightful experiences, of the beastly transport conditions in the cattle cars without food or water. A Dutch witness during the Eichmann trials recalled one such journey:

> The sick, the aged and babies in arms were crushed into barred cattle trucks... They had been aboard the trains for two days and had only once received food. She (a Jewish refugee) said that some babies had suffocated in the crush and that the SS guards had even then forced in more people and bolted the door.

Who decided which Jews were to go to what camp? Who decided which Jews were allowed to go to those 'different camps', Bergen Belsen and Theresienstadt? This was *Referat* IV B 4 (the so-called *Judenreferat* – Jews Office) of the *Reichssicherheitshauptamt* (State Security Main Office), the Gestapo office on the Kurfürstenstrasse 15/16 in Berlin, where Adolf Eichmann and his staff coordinated the logistics of the murder of the Jews. They held dossiers with all sorts of administrative data about the Jews of Europe and their confiscated assets. Eichmann had representatives in every country whose special assignment was to relieve the Jews of their posses-

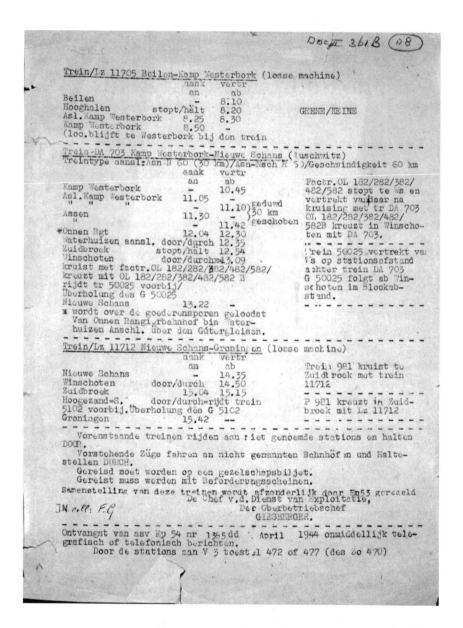

Time table Westerbork-Auschwitz

sions and transport them to Poland. Making the transport arrangements was no easy matter: extra trains had to be wrestled from their military priorities and had to be scheduled under increasingly difficult circumstances.[2] There was paperwork concerning the crossing of borders, there was the matter of fares. Neither the *Nederlandsche Spoorwegen* (Dutch Railways) nor the *Deutsche Reichsbahn* (German Railways) were inclined to transport these extra passengers for free: both charged Eichmann's office the price of a one-way ticket(!) for every adult passenger, children up to the age of ten had to pay half price, and only children up to four years of age could travel free.

The journeys could take a long time. Destination Sobibor meant a train journey of at least three days, Auschwitz and Theresienstadt were usually reached after two days, and Bergen-Belsen after one.

Bergen-Belsen

Bergen-Belsen, situated between Hamburg and Hannover on the Lüneburger Heath, was a so-called *Aufenthaltslager* (stopover camp). Jews were kept there who might be exchanged at some stage for Germans in foreign countries, or who had important contacts (business or otherwise) in neutral or Allied countries from which Germany hoped to profit at some stage.

Abel Herzberg, with a so-called Palestine certificate which qualified Jews for an exchange transport, describes how they were tossed about between hope and despair every time they looked forward to departing from Bergen-Belsen, only to have that hope thwarted at the last moment. In the end, only three smallish transports of a couple of hundred people each made it out of Germany, among which was a transport of 222 Dutch Jews to Palestine at the end of June 1944.

All in all, almost 4000 Jews from Holland were taken to Bergen-Belsen. There, Loden Vogel, a young medical student from Amsterdam, met Renata Laqueur and Philip Mechanicus, whom he had considered a 'kindred spirit' in Westerbork.

Mechanicus would be transported from Bergen-Belsen to Auschwitz in September 1944 together with more than 100 other Dutch Jews. There he was shot in one of the crematoriums of Birkenau. He was therefore spared the last terrible months of Bergen-Belsen. Only 1100 Dutchmen would survive this 'camp of the privileged'.

In comparison with other camps, the regime could be described as reasonable until the autumn of 1944. It depended to a large degree on the labour detail an individual was assigned to; unlucky ones might have to work for 11 hours. But it also depended on the nature of the persons' relationship with the kapos[3], and on their ability to 'organise' (camp jargon for being able to lay hands on food and cigarettes, a euphemism for stealing). In all camps there was a great deal of bartering, with cigarettes valued as the highest commodity. Another very important rule of survival was: be inconspicuous.

*

Until the autumn of 1944, life in Bergen-Belsen was relatively bearable. Jona Oberski, who was 6 years old when he entered the camp, tells how it was possible for his parents to see each other intimately on occasion. But the often lust-laden atmosphere of Westerbork, where, as Herzberg wrote, *people used to couple with sensuous, mindless abandon,* was long gone. Here, most sexual relations were not without self-interest. Loden Vogel writes:

> Yesterday I heard what a girl can earn by going to bed with Hanke (chief-kapo): a loaf of bread, a pound of butter, a sausage, a 'good meal.' But only once. I would do it, if I were a pretty girl. Lots of them do. (Vogel, 1965:134, own translation)

Renata Laqueur likewise did not want to condemn those women and even envied them for their 'courage':

> I was not so brave as to make that step. I did not know where it would end…And I had lots of invitations, even from the highest ranks. (Laqueur, 1965:103, own translation)

There would be less and less time for quick flirtations, even for emotions. Herzberg:

> Dull, dull, dull, that's what life is like here…It is as if the elixir of life has dried up and that all that is left is hunger…No love is here, no eros…There are no relationships and if there are, they are confined to superficial admiration. Children do not understand any more that men and women can sleep differently than separately in barracks. They have forgotten the bedroom of their parents. They hardly remember what it is like to live in a house… And yet as men and women are getting closer, they put their head on each others' shoulder, out of a terrible fear for loneliness (...)
> Don't leave me alone, that's what they seem to say (...) Life has become ghostly. The fire is burning, but it is cold. And the light throws no shadows. It is as if we are made of glass, just as transparent, just as fragile. Love has left us. (Herzberg, 1950: 124 and 126; own translation)

These sentences show remarkable similarities with the comments of David Koker in Vught; he is amazed at the way emotions seem to have drained away:

> Our whole life here is formal, in fact. Our relationship to people: an empty shell from which the live contents have been taken away…People become of glass here, as it were. They keep everything they had in the old days, but as if in a museum. (Koker, 1977:126; own translation)

Loden Vogel has similar observations, even though he also saw another side:

Very seldom is somebody here really interested in somebody else. Only: good marriages get even better. Family ties become stronger: grown up brothers and sisters help each other. Consequently corruption is not so immoral... (Vogel, 1965:79; own translation)

Generally speaking, Vogel did not have a very high opinion of his fellow prisoners. Where so many were pre-occupied with the one single act of surviving, it does seem a very harsh judgment:

So few of them show any understanding for what is really tragic in their condition, that they don't have the right to be called martyrs anymore. If ever anybody had that right, of course, and martyr is not the right word. They have no sense of adventure, or they die like cackling chickens, that represents it better. I don't feel like writing anymore, most certainly not describing. (Vogel, 1965:20-21; own translation)

This detached tone of the medical student who analyzed everything, may point to a psychological defence mechanism that occurred frequently in the camps, called 'acute depersonalization' by physician Elie Cohen in his dissertation, *The German Concentration Camp* (1952), which is one of the first psychological studies on the subject. This depersonalization caused a personality split that enabled the author to distance himself: reality being too terrible to be experienced directly.

*

During the last months of the war, circumstances in the camp deteriorated rapidly. The overflowing camp was daily swamped with new prisoner transports: every day, 50 to 100 people were left behind dead after each roll-call. Herzberg and Laqueur both wrote about the daily torture of the endless counting during roll-call:

If it does not tally, we will be standing in the evening for another couple of hours on an empty stomach in the freezing cold. [After evening roll-call] there are the precious moments when one tries to be 'a human being' and to remember that the world does not consist entirely of beating, cursing, orders and swearing. That is the moment when one tries not to think about the dreadful hunger and to realise that it will all end well and that the war will be over soon. (Laqueur, 1965:36, own translation)

Renata Laqueur was too weak at the end of 1944 to continue to write in her diary. The final wave came in early 1945, when the Nazis shipped a good part of the population of Auschwitz to Belsen's already overcrowded barracks. Epidemics (typhoid, typhus, dysentery) caused the heaps of corpses Bergen-Belsen is so notorious for; nobody had enough strength left to bury them. All sources tell about the battle against the degradation of the human body through filthiness, disease, vermin (lice), hunger and cold during those last months. Many lost that battle. Five hundred inmates died every day. Mirjam Blits, who arrived in Bergen-Belsen from Auschwitz in November 1944, described what happened after their arrival in the worst part of the camp:

> We asked the other girls [...] where we could find a place to wash. They took us to an open field, a piece of bare heathland. An iron pipe was running through it with holes every ten centimeter or so. Water came out of these holes and ran straight into the ground. Who had enough courage to get undressed in the ice-cold November wind and wash? We did not have towels, so one couldn't dry oneself. We didn't even talk about soap. But I felt so filthy and dirty with lice that were crawling over my body, that I plucked up the courage to get completely undressed and give myself a wash in the freezing water. I had to be careful in the meantime that my shirt and pants were not made 'klepsy klepsy' ('klepsy' comes from the Greek word for 'thieving'). (Blits, 1961:248, own translation)

Loden Vogel has written about the food-fantasies, a familiar phenomenon for anyone who has been in a camp situation. He decribes how the inmates could sit and phantasise for hours about everything they were going to eat after the war and about all the meals they had had before war broke out. Juxtaposing the drives of hunger and sex, he wrote: *I would like to read a cookbook just as I used to read pornography.* (Vogel, 1965:133)

Josef Weiss emigrated to Holland in 1933 and came via Westerbork to Bergen-Belsen. In his report on Bergen-Belsen, written just after the war, he describes in great detail the consequences of hunger and filth. Among other things, he mentions one of the last taboos of life in the concentration camps: cannibalism.[4] As the Nazis had cut off the food supply entirely, we cannot be surprised to read about its occurrence.

*

The notorious camp commander, SS-Hauptsturmführer Josef Kramer, previously in charge at Auschwitz must be held responsible for many of the deaths at Bergen-Belsen as well. Abel Herzberg paints in *Amor Fati* a psychological portrait of the commanders and kapos of Bergen-Belsen. Although written just after the war, these portraits are remarkably penetrating, far beyond mere hatefulness.[5] A good example is the paragraph he devotes to Fräulein Gertrud Slottke, a notorious SS official in The Hague and a visitor of Bergen-Belsen, who decided which Jews with a *Sperre* could nevertheless be deported:

> Our very own Fräulein Slottke, with her tawny, fanatical face, whom we shall always remember as a nightmare come to life. She was of stone, presumably frozen by a perverse loneliness, an empty parchment bag, ideal hiding-place for the devil who possessed her. Over what was probably her breast she wore a

crimson decoration, a carmine order, the emblem of her distinguished service during the dejudification of Europe. A witch who, unfeelingly, filed and sorted the 'material' and saw to it that the goods were dispatched on time to the East. Sometimes something trembled on her upper lip, something like holy satisfaction, when she saw the despair she caused in women when they were separated from their husbands, in children separated from their mothers. Children whom she hated, because she had none of her own, happiness which she destroyed because she herself was without it. Fräulein Slottke was spiteful. (Herzberg, 1965:31, own translation)

Jona Oberski, now a Dutch physicist, saw his parents die in Bergen-Belsen. In his book *Childhood*, there are phrases that are almost impossible to read. They have to be read, nevertheless. He visits his dying father in the hospital for what is going to be the last time:

It was really my father. I recognised his closed eyelids, his nose, his mouth and his ears. His cheeks were thin, but they were still like my father's cheeks, the way I'd known them early in the morning in bed; my father who had held me on his lap, who had let me ride horseback on his knee. (...) He heaved a deep sigh and opened his eyes. He looked surprised, but the doctor had told us that he'd been asleep when they brought him in. So he probably didn't know where he was. He opened his mouth wide to say something. But then a funny thing happened: he couldn't get it closed again. He wanted to say something, but he couldn't. (Oberski, 1983:70/71)

After he had watched his father die, he tried to find him the next day in the boilerhouse of the camp. Amid a heap of bodies, he observes something that resembles his father:

I went in and stepped over the first bodies. I climbed up on the pile and looked into the topmost bundled sheet. All I could see was an arm. I started to unwrap the sheet.(...) I pulled out the arm. The hand was like my father's. I tugged at the sheet until I could see the face. The face was black with beard. I climbed down off the pile and saw a body to the side. It wasn't getting much light. I looked at the face. The eyes were black. The cheeks were thin. The beard was short like my father's. The nose was like his, too. I looked at the hands. They were like my father's. But the body wasn't at all like my father's. (Oberski, 1983:78/79)

Bergen-Belsen was liberated on 15 April 1945 by the British Army. Finding huge mountains of dead and dying that looked nothing like human beings, the British could think of no other solution than to dig large mass graves and bulldoze the dead bodies into them.[6] Of the survivors, about 13,000 lost their lives after liberation, through disease or plain exhaustion like Oberski's mother, Durlacher's father and Laqueur's sister.

"Large graves were dug and the bodies bulldozed into them"

Keeping up Appearances: Theresienstadt

Theresienstadt, situated not far from Prague, was initially a transit camp for Czech Jews, then in addition became a so-called *Altersghetto* (ghetto for the elderly). The Germans proclaimed that certain categories of Jews would be sent there instead of straight to the extermination camps:

- (German) Jews over 65 years old.

- (German) Jews who had received a military decoration (Iron Cross or higher) in the First World War or had given meritorious service to Germany at some time or another.

This reflected in every way the divide-and-rule policy of the Nazis: the Jews would do anything to be sent to this exceptional camp, to avoid the unknown camps in the East. It was also held out as a reward to the leadership of the Jewish Councils. The two chairmen of the Dutch Jewish Council, Asscher and Cohen, were sent with their families and some 4500 other Jews from Holland to Theresienstadt. Many of those were eventually – later in 1944 – sent on to Auschwitz, among them young Gerard Durlacher.

As Mechanicus knew already in Westerbork:

Hitler wants to exterminate the Jews. He has said so more than once. Yet he calls for the Jews in trains fit for human beings and takes them to a favoured spot in Europe: Theresienstadt. He exterminates them in separate classes, just as a firm of undertakers buries its dead clients according to different categories (...) Hitler is playing the part of the undertaker and he takes off his hat to Jews who occupied priviliged positions in their lifetime. (Mechanicus, 1968:230-231)

In addition, Theresienstadt was used by the Nazis as a *Propagandalager* (propaganda camp) that could be shown to a worried outside world. As a show camp it was allowed to develop many cultural activities, such as lectures, music concerts, theatre performances and sports.[7] Music, art and theater were part of the life in Theresienstadt, just as in Westerbork – the little town was not much larger than the camp – but here with more human talent from all over Europe. The artistic activity in this antechamber to Auschwitz was impressive. Jacob Edelstein, the first Elder of the Jews (appointed by the Germans), established a Youth Welfare Department (Jugendfürsorge) for the children, who accounted for about 10% of the population of Theresienstadt, and this organised some (illegal) education.

Durlacher, in his memoirs *Stripes in the Sky*, calls Theresienstadt a 'privileged' concentration camp. What was hidden behind the façade becomes clear when one reads the survivor's testimonies. One of them describes minutely how the camp was everything but a 'spa', where the elderly could look forward to a trouble-free retirement. The struggle for life was just as fierce, the contrasts just as obvious as in the 'ordinary' camps. In total, something like 141,000 Jews came to Theresienstadt, 23% of them died here, the large majority of the remainder were later sent on to other camps, in particular Auschwitz, and died there.

The Jews from Holland had been presented with a sunny picture of Theresienstadt. When the first transport was announced, Hauptsturm-führer Aus der Fünten stressed that *the ladies have to make sure they bring sturdy shoes for the outings*. Only 1300 survived the excursion.

Unlike the Red Cross of other countries, the Dutch Red Cross in London refused to send food parcels to the Dutch Jews in Theresienstadt; they considered the risk that these would fall into the wrong hands too great and decided to do nothing.

*

The outside world became familiar with this propaganda camp in different ways. In June 1944 representatives of the Danish Red Cross and the International Red Cross visited the site that had been spruced up for the occasion. During the visit a concert was given, a play was performed, sports were played, but the members of the delegation had no chance to speak to Jews at random. The delegation allowed itself to be fooled and deceived by all this. Fred Schwarz, who arrived in Theresienstadt late in 1944, talked to a woman who had seen how the delegation had been wrongfooted every time: *They have been here in the ghetto for six hours, walked the exact route the SS had set out for them and have not said a word to anybody outside the protocol, nor looked behind any curtain.* (Schwarz, 1994:191, own translation)

The same props were used for the next propaganda stunt. The movie universally known as *Der Führer schenkt den Juden eine Stadt* (Hitler Gives the Jews a City)[8] was also meant to mislead world opinion. The director was Kurt Gerron, a famous movie and cabaret star in Berlin in the Twenties, who had come to Theresienstadt from Westerbork. One of his collaborators was Dutch artist Jo Spier. Professor David Cohen, chairman of the Jewish Council, was one of the actors. Durlacher comments:

> During the weeks of the filming, between 16 August and 11 September 1944, Theresienstadt was a grotesque movie studio with spectators in black uniforms and caps with death's head insignias commanding the movie-makers and actors and admonishing them to remember their mortality. The privileged artists believed themselves safe and indispensable. For two weeks, the black uniformed illusionists of mercy kept the fantasy alive by granting gifts and favours. In the weeks between 28 September and 28 October 1944, 17,520 film-makers, actors and extras journeyed to the terminus that was Auschwitz. Only 1496 returned. Kurt Gerron was not one of them. For services rendered, he was given Special Treatment with cyanide gas immediately upon arrival.(Durlacher, 1991:69).

The movie (Durlacher called it a 'cynical comedy') was never officially released, although it was shown by the SS to visiting members of rescue committees in early April 1945. Parts of the film were found by a Czech civilian in a burnt-out truck of the German army in May 1945.

The Empire of Death: Auschwitz-Birkenau

Although situated in a remote and hidden corner of southwest Poland, the village of Oswiecim (Auschwitz) was an important railway junction. After the occupation of Poland in 1939, the Germans used the old Polish army barracks to house Russian prisoners of war. This lasted until the summer of 1942. After Himmler's ambitious plans for a German model city were shelved, Auschwitz was to be given a new function.[9] More or less created out of necessity, it became the most important and largest extermination camp from the middle of 1942 onwards. In the fall of 1941 and the spring of 1942, a new large camp was built, about three kilometers from the old camp. Known as Auschwitz II (Birkenau), this was the actual extermination camp with many barracks, surrounded by high-voltage barbed wire, a guard house and watchtowers.

Daily, the cattle trucks would arrive from all parts of Europe. It is estimated that Birkenau 'housed' at its peak, in 1943, 150,000 prisoners. The individual barracks, built for 500 prisoners, sometimes held as many as 1000. In the camp, prisoners were forced to build large gas chambers and crematoriums, according to SS specifications and under the supervision of German firms. Without its architects and engineers, Auschwitz would never have grown into the kind of destruction machine where the killing of one prisoner cost only 0.25 Mark.

After a long journey that could last anything between two and four days riding across Europe, the long row of cattle cars reached their destination. On top of the uncertainty of the journey came the bitter cold of winter or the stifling heat of summer. Usually the trip was made without food or water, with one bucket serving 70 or 80 people as a toilet. That bucket was usually full after one hour, causing great embarrassment for everybody who needed to use it. It was only the beginning of a process of degradation and dehumanization. From Holland around 60,000 Jews were transported to Auschwitz, and in 1944, 234 gypsies were also taken there.[10]

*

It was always the same train travelling to and fro between Westerbork and Auschwitz. People began to hide little messages and notes in small cracks between the planks for those who had stayed behind in Westerbork. A few of those messages have been preserved: they talk about the atmosphere in the wagon during the journey, it was *terrible, everybody is bitchy and argues,* or *fine: we had a cabaret the first evening and sang songs,* we hear about a barber who shaved the men and about a teacher *who spoke about Zionism so interestingly that we completely forgot where we were going,* but the last sentence was often something like this:

> We are standing still in Auschwitz, we have to get out. It is a large industrial town, because I can see many chimneys or: In the distance I can see a brightly-lit building. So long guys, we'll be back soon. (Mak, 1995:280/281, own translation)

We are well-informed about the selection procedure that followed: one of the books that has documented the whole journey thoroughly is Willy Lindwer's *The Last Seven Months of Anne Frank.* It tells of the experiences of six women, all of whom knew Anne Frank at one stage or another after the arrest of the eight people in the hiding-place. But the book is about much more than Anne Frank: it contains the complete interviews from a documentary film of the same title and, as such, is a testimony to incredible experiences, told in the most sober way. Janny Brandes-Brilleslijper describes the confusing effect of the neon lights and the loudspeakers at the platform of Auschwitz-Birkenau like this:

> It was a voice that shouted, 'Alles austreten, alle Bagage hinlegen' (everybody out, put down your luggage), 'women to one side, men to the other side. Women and children who can't walk, go to the trucks that are waiting for you.' The

horrible effect of that very bright, dirty-looking neon light, a bluish light, and that gray sky above, more or less lit up by the neon lamps. And those little men in blue striped suits, who whispered, 'Ihr seid gesund. Lauf.' (You are healthy. Walk) They were trying to warn us. We didn't understand any of it. (Lindwer, 1991:56)

Usually the ones who chose to take the trucks were driven straight to the gas chambers – among them, in any case, all people over 50 and under 15. The others had to undergo a humiliating selection procedure, whereby the ones that were deemed fit for work were separated from the unfit-looking ones. The latter were taken to the gas chambers straight away as well. Everything took place at a fast pace, meant to leave noone time to think or collect his/her thoughts. It appears as if this confusion was created deliberatedly: when the train arrived early, while it was still light, it would wait on a siding until it could arrive in the dark; people were harrassed to leave the train in a great hurry; the neon lights, the loudspeakers, the 'schnell, schnell, schnell' of the guards, the barking of dogs, it all served the same purpose: to throw people off balance. Ronnie Goldstein-van Cleef illustrates this point when she tells about her impressions just after her arrival in Auschwitz-Birkenau:

> While we were all standing there in separate groups, men and women mixed together, my uncle came up to me and said, "Do you know where Suze is?"
> "I just saw her, but I don't see her now. But I'll go and ask one of the men in striped suits." Those were Dutchmen who had already been there for a very long time.
> I asked one of them and got the answer, "They are already dead," as if that were quite natural. I said, "That isn't possible; I just saw her." I couldn't take it in at all. I thought, that man is not all there. (Lindwer, 1991: 180)

It was virtually impossible to escape from this camp. There was a permanent garrison of more than 2000 heavily armed SS soldiers. The 800 Jews of the 'Sonderkommando' (Special Detail) knew that, too. They had to accompany the victims to the gas chamber, hand them a towel and a piece of soap, lead them to the showers, where Zyklon-B (prussic acid) brought about a quick asphyxiation. It was then up to the Sonderkommandos to bring the bodies from the gas chamber to the crematoriums and burn them. Every three months the members of the Sonderkommando were gassed themselves. In October 1944 one of the teams smuggled in dynamite and a few guns: they blew up one of the gas chambers and killed about 70 SS soldiers. Twelve men escaped and hid with a Polish farmer but were betrayed immediately, brought back and killed with all the others.

Those who passed the selection on the platform and had not been referred to 'the other side', entered the camp and often smelled the stench of burnt flesh. Eva Schloss, acquainted with the Frank family, came with her mother to the women's part of the Birkenau camp in the summer of 1944. She describes the welcome they received from a (female) kapo:

> "Can you smell the camp crematorium?" she shouted viciously. "That's where your dear relatives have been gassed in what they thought were shower rooms. They're burning now. You'll never see them again!" We tried not to listen. She was just trying to frighten us. We did not believe her; it was simply too terrible to contemplate. (Schloss, 1988:74)

After the first registration another humiliating ritual took place. In order to treat the Jews as 'subhumans', it was considered necessary to rob them of their individuality. Robbed of their hair and subjected to extreme under-nourishment, men and women looked almost indistinguishable. To dehumanise them, the Germans denied the very existence of a prisoner's name, tattooing each with a number on their left arm.

One of those undergoing this process of subhumanization was Gerard Durlacher; he describes how they had to line up for what looked like another registration:

> On these tables: paper, ink, pens. But how different and frightening the use of these simple writing implements is. One striped figure notes our names and other relevant information and calls out a number, and a second grabs my left arm and rapidly tattoos a letter and a number. From now on, I am A-1321. Many people have their number crossed out with the needles and replaced by another. The administrative competence can be read on our arms. Every prick burns in our brains, and woe be unto him who does not know his new 'name' perfectly. (Durlacher, 1991:50)

Before work could start, the 'lucky' inmates who had survived the selection so far had to undergo one more moment of degradation:

> Stocky striped figures with gleaming shaved craniums take charge of us. We undress under threats and oaths and an occasional beating. I try to put my shoes in a place where I can find them again, the shoelaces tied to each other. The razor scrapes cruelly across my lower abdomen. Our pubic hair and the hair from the heads of some of the boys falls to the floor. On a sign on the wall, I read "Eine Laus, dein Tod" (a louse means your death). Our shame dies. Even the order "Bucken und Arsch hoch" (bend over with your ass in the air) doesn't matter any more. Only the fear of pain remains. We enter the showers and hear the bath Kapos utter their crude jokes about gas or our physiques. We try to remain passive. By making the water ice cold or scalding hot, the Kapos are able to prolong their enjoyment a little longer. (Durlacher, 1991:57-58)

Those who had passed the selection by the SS doctors were kept in reserve for hard labour in the camp itself – *seconds later, they're pushing overloaded wheelbarrows, shoveling sand, scrubbing latrines or sweeping the dusty camp roads* (Durlacher, 1991:51) – in the satellite camp of Monowitz or in one of its 39 *Nebenlager* (subsidiary camps). German industrial firms like AEG and IG Farben were some of the main beneficiaries from this cheap labour supply. The average life expectancy of a Jew who was not immediately gassed on arrival was between six and seven weeks in Auschwitz. Towards the end of the war, the situation improved somewhat because by then the Germans needed every hand.

Polish writer Tadeusz Borowski in his bitingly ironic *This Way for the Gas, Ladies and Gentlemen* recalled: *It is an unwritten law of the camp that people who are on their way to their death are deceived unto the last moment. That is the only permitted show of sympathy.* Thus, the prisoners were told they had to take a shower to be disinfected and therefore had to undress in one of the barracks. Then they had to go naked into the gas chambers.[11] The doors were then sealed, and the gas shaken down through the holes. Camp commandant Rudolf Hoess said during his trial in Nuremberg:

> At Auschwitz, I used Zyklon-B, which was a crystallized prussic acid which we dropped into the death chamber from a small opening. It took from 3 to 15 minutes to kill the people in the death chamber, depending on the climatic conditions. We knew the people were dead because their screaming stopped.

Hoess calculated that at least 2.5 million people lost their lives in the gas chambers of Auschwitz-Birkenau and that on top of that, half a million died through disease and starvation. Later, it was estimated that at least 1 million Jews lost their lives in Auschwitz.

What did the executioners think about their work? Himmler had heartened them in Poznan on 14 October 1943 in this way:

> Most of you must know what it means when 100 corpses are lying side by side or 500 or 1000. To have stuck it out and at the same time – apart from exceptions caused by human weakness – to have remained decent fellows, that is what has made us hard. This is a page of glory in our history, which has never been written and is never to be written.

Hoess wrote after the war, before he was hanged in a Polish prison: *I was no longer happy in Auschwitz, once the mass exterminations had begun* (Auschwitz, 1994:80). That does not alter the fact that he still did his job meticulously for two and a half years, while his wife busied herself by having the flower garden tended by camp inmates.[12] A survivor wrote: *Death was as familiar to us as a landscape where one lives and grows up. He belonged with us like the air that we breathed.* Everywhere danger lurked, it could strike unexpectedly at any moment. The random selections were the most dangerous. Elie Cohen tells of an incident that involved an acquaintance of his, *a healthy, sturdy fellow*, who suddenly found himself among those that had been selected for the gas chamber:

I asked him what had happened, he answered with one word: 'Organisation'. He had not been selected, but a friend of the Polish barrack clerk had. The clerk had taken the number of his friend off the list and written the number of the Dutchman in its place. The Germans were only concerned about the number; appeal was impossible. We looked silently at one another. Presently he said: "That's Auschwitz for you", turned around and walked away. He went towards his death, I was permitted to live. (Cohen, 1992:92; own translation)

*

The fate of the Dutch Jews was not essentially different from that of Jews from other countries. But there seem to have been minor differences. Somehow, the Jews from Holland seemed less capable of adapting to the harsh circumstances of camp life. Maybe they had lived a life of relative peace and comfort for too long, maybe their bourgeois values could not stand up against the free-for-all of life in the camps, where in order to survive oneself, one had to watch others die. Jules Schelvis, himself a survivor of Sobibor, blames the level of assimilation of Dutch Jews. In a conversation with some Polish labourers, he remarks:

We told long stories about our work and about our families, about Amsterdam and Holland, how we lived and worked there and felt Dutch in the first place, in despite of being Jewish. In Poland Jews are not Poles, but second rate citizens. They did not consider as self-evident, like we did, that we were accepted as ordinary Dutchmen in Dutch society and were treated as equals. They listened to us with disbelief. (Schelvis, 1982:59, own translation)

The historian Louis de Jong elucidates the different attitude of the Dutch Jews:

Jews from The Netherlands found it more difficult than other Jews to fight for a crust of bread or a spoonful of soup or a less bone-breaking job. Their decency was their undoing.
  In the period from July 1942 to February 1943, from all transports from Westerbork camp, on average 160 male deportees were not sent immediately to the gas chambers but were shipped either to Auschwitz I or to Auschwitz II, Birkenau. In Birkenau alone there were nights, immediately following their arrival in the camp, when 30 of these 160 male deportees committed suicide, mostly by throwing themselves on the barbed wire of the electrified fence. Figures for the cases of suicide among Dutch Jews are significantly higher than similar figures for Jews from other countries. (De Jong, 1990:23)

One of the first after the war to describe her experiences in Auschwitz was Mirjam Blits, who dedicated her memoirs of Auschwitz to her mother *who voluntarily took my place in the gas chamber*. In shrill, unadulterated terms she writes about life in the camp. Consigned to the women's camp of Birkenau, she asked herself the same question: why was it that Dutch men and women perished so quickly in Auschwitz? Her answer comes close to De Jong's 'their decency was their undoing' when she blames the Dutch inability to flatter people in command. *To go up to an SS woman and flatter her, no Dutch woman could do that* (p.222), and she explains that it was for this reason that Dutch Jewesses were called 'crazy' in all the camps (*Blöde Holländerinnen*). During a nightly trip to the latrines with a bucket full of excrement she stumbles and falls. Lying in the shit and the mud, she comes close to giving up:

> Never before had I felt so unhappy as that night. While the sky was red with the flames, rising from the recently swept chimneys, and the Camp was stinking of the corpses, I prayed: God, please, let me die, I don't want to go on. Let me also go through the chimney. Dear God, I don't want to continue. (Blits, 1961:219; own translation)

The physician Elie Cohen admits that he had it slightly easier as a doctor, but for him as well, adaptation was inevitable:

> I did not particularly like being in charge of the shithouse ('Scheisshausmeister' is the word he uses) and to have to clean the toilets. When I cleaned blocked toilets with my bare hands, I felt it as an humiliation: but one had to have a certain survival instinct, not in the usual sense of the word, but as a defense mechanism that would enable one to laugh about these things. The only thing one could do was to resign oneself to it, try and make the best of it and get through. It was very important not to feel sorry for yourself and even more important not to have others feel sorry for you, because then you were in a bad way. (Cohen, 1992:73; own translation)

Some tried to escape, were caught and hanged, while other inmates were compelled to watch. Eva Schloss recalls: *None of us saw the hanging. We were forced to look – but we did not see* (Schloss, 1988:92), and Durlacher also speaks of *non-seeing eyes*.

The many reports of meetings with the dreaded Dr Josef Mengele breathe fear and horror. He decided over life and death every day, with a flick of the hand or a single word. Menachem Arnoni, a Polish-Jewish survivor who would later become known for his unorthodox political visions, portrayed Mengele in a bitterly sardonic light, in a book called *Moeder was niet thuis voor haar begrafenis* (Mother Was Not Home for Her Funeral):

> Is he capable of love? For a woman, children, parents? For people in general? Of course. And yet he sends people like those to their deaths? Absolutely, and he does it out of love. (Arnoni, 1982:224, own translation)

Durlacher, lined up for a selection, saw him approach: *With every rejection, I stand straighter, my fists at my side, my head made of granite. He walks past and leaves me alone.* (Durlacher, 1991:56) He survived Mengele's selections together with 89 other boys between 13 and 16 years of age. He differed from another inmate of Auschwitz, Primo Levi, in that he never saw life in the camp as a war of all against all. He prefers to remember the spirit of sacrifice, though rare, even among the perpetrators: *At the nadir of every civilisation, a residue of decency is left*, he says.[13] And Presser confirms that the material abounds with examples of human solidarity, of kindliness, sympathy and compassion, *the flowers on this dungheap*, as someone has called them.

But Levi's point of view seems to have been shared by many others who returned from the camp. Mirjam Blits' experiences in Auschwitz come very close to Levi's. She writes about civilization as *our thin layer of veneer* and continues:

> It is easy to be nice and good and sociable in times of freedom (...) But the fight for every scrap of food, the fight to remain healthy, the fight for the few pieces of clothing (...). To have to fight always and everywhere, twenty-four hours per day, even in your sleep, when exhaustion has taken over, when you lie down with a piece of string around your wrist, a little bag attached to it with everything you own in it, thinking: everything might get stolen during the night and then to wake up in the morning to find only the piece of string around your wrist. The rest has been cut off. Gone. Where is our civilization when we are in trouble? (Blits, 1961:211; own translation)

Mengele not only made selections, he also conducted gruesome medical experiments without anaesthetics. He had a particular interest in using twins in his pseudo-scientific research. He wanted to 'prove' the superiority of the Nordic race. Once he killed single-handedly 16 young gypsy twins with a shot in the back of the neck, because he wanted to have their inner organs measured accurately.

Another gruesome topic is the camp orchestra.'*Murder with music*', writes Presser, *is perhaps a fitting description of this twentieth century* danse macabre - *whenever people were marched to the gas chambers, or about to be hanged, the band would strike up*. A Dutch physician has described the camp orchestra: *The flautist was a Greek gynaecologist who, on one occasion, was still playing while his own daughter rode past in a lorry, on her way to the gas chamber.* (Presser, 1969:508)

The writers also make us familiar with the mass clearances of corpses – as the removing of gold teeth from the corpses' mouths – and the sorting barracks ('Kanada') – where all the luggage, left on the platform, and all the personal belongings were sorted.[14]

*

Probably in early November 1944 Himmler stopped the gassings. He apparently wanted a position from which to negotiate with the Allied Armies and hoped to convince them that communism was the real enemy.[15] He made an effort to erase the gas chambers and crematoria, but while the sound of gunfire was getting nearer all the time, and the SS guards were getting more and more nervous, many people were dying of starvation and disease. Durlacher remembers how he used rations that were meant for others who had no use for them anymore:

> ...when a disembodied hand proffers a piece of bread, I take my neighbor's portion as well, for he's gone to a place where food doesn't count anymore. From the land of the dead, he saves my life. I play this game of resurrection two or three times, but when only a few of my companions in the lower bunks are still alive, I flee this underworld, and with my last ounce of strength I hoist my lice-infected and scabies-ridden body to the upper bunk. (Durlacher, 1991:74)

Many tens of thousands would still perish before the Red Army finally liberated Auschwitz and Birkenau on 27 January 1945.

Sobibor

In three other extermination camps – Belzec, Sobibor and Treblinka – 1.5 to 1.7 million Jews were murdered in assembly-line fashion in 1942/1943. This top-secret operation was called *Aktion Reinhard*, 'to honour' Reinhard Heydrich, one of the masterminds of the *Endlösung der Judenfrage* (Final Solution of the Jewish Problem), who had died in June 1942 as a result of a successful action by Czech partisans.[16] Many of those involved in the mass murder of the *Aktion Reinhard* had used the experience they had gained during the large 'Euthanasia' program, in which at least 70,000 mentally and physically handicapped Germans had been murdered, between 1939 and 1941.[17] This was all part of the policy of 'racial purity'.

Between March and July 1943, more than 34,000 Jews from Holland arrived in Sobibor, in the east of Poland. Almost all of them were immediately gassed on arrival.

Clara Spits, who survived the war by going into hiding in Friesland, left Holland in 1946 for South Africa. There she began to write under the name of Clarissa Jacobi. One of her stories is called *A Real Kavalsky*. While in hospital in Cape Town after the birth of her child, Dutch war survivor Esther Kavalsky is visited by her Aunt Bessie, an Auschwitz survivor. Esther is crying uncontrollably; the reader recognises the symptoms of post-natal depression, but Aunt Bessie has another explanation:

"Ach, Esther, you don't need to tell me anything. You don't have to put on an act for me...You're all the time thinking about your mother, about your parents...When a woman goes through childbirth, she longs for her mother. Nobody else will do...You want to show your mother the baby, see the joy on her face...Your parents, I never wanted to ask you the details, did they also take them to Auschwitz?" "To Sobibor!" "To Sobibor! In Auschwitz one still had a very slight chance. If one was young and strong, that is, and with the necessary little bit of mazzel. If one can call it mazzel. Sometimes it was better to die quickly than to go through such hell. In Sobibor everybody could say the Shema (prayer to be recited before dying). The survivors from that camp could be counted on one hand." (Jacobi, 1972:53/54)

Only 19 Dutch people in total would survive Sobibor. For one of them, Jules Schelvis, it was not sufficient just to write down his memories of this camp. Jules Schelvis felt he was called upon to write the first academic study about this relatively unknown extermination camp, after having been present at the trial of the henchmen of Sobibor in Germany in the Eighties. Schelvis describes how the Dutch prisoners were forced to write enthusiastic letters home about the camp, saying 'I am very well', and that the barracks in Sobibor resembled houses in the Austrian Alps and had names like 'Lustige Flo' (The Lusty Flea), 'Gottes Heimat' (God's Home) and 'Schwalbennest' (Swallows Nest). The Jewish Council in Amsterdam fell for it and is reported to have been relieved that the Jews were doing so well in Sobibor.

Another form of deception was the speeches of SS-Oberscharführer Michel, who told the recently arrived Jews with great sincerity that this camp was a transit camp en route to the Ukraine, where they were going to work under Jewish supervision. Even Polish Jews, who on the whole had very few illusions left about the intentions of the Nazis, applauded. Half an hour later they were all dead.

The climax of Schelvis' book is the chapter on the 'courage of despair': the rebellion in the camp in October 1943. The large majority of escaping prisoners were mowed down by German machine guns. One day after the rebellion, not one Jew remained alive in Sobibor. Those who had not fled were executed. It is the only time Schelvis raises his voice: *They wanted to do everything in their power to teach the arrogant Herrenvolk, murderers of millions, an unforgettable lesson.* Shortly after this rebellion, Sobibor was abandoned and razed to the ground. In August 1943 a rebellion of the Sonderkommando in Treblinka against the SS met with a similar fate, and Treblinka was destroyed in the autumn of 1943.

Jewish author Maurits Mok (1907-1989) was obsessed by the destruction of the Jews. His novels and poetry are characterised by an effort to identify with the victims of the Nazi era. It is almost as if he is trying to communicate with the murdered. He recorded his memories of the violated Jewish neighbourhood of Amsterdam. In his poem *Sobibor*, he writes:

Between earth and heaven
furnaces of death stand
like prehistoric animals.
Six hundred people, beaten
out of the light, keep the desperate red
of their gaping mouths wide open to the poison
that fills the space like a cloudburst.

The hundreds, with gagging lungs,
mill their arms around in the stifled air
and scream till their veins burst.
Then they still hang, with gaping mouths,
dead round each other's throats.

Bystanders

The Dutch government, in exile in London since May 1940, seemed not particularly interested in the fate of the deported Jews, a lack of interest common to all the Allied governments. From the spring of 1942, the representative of the World Jewish Congress in Geneva, Gerhard Riegner, had continuously informed the Allied governments of the gassings in Poland. He was not believed. When in the summer of 1942 ever more persistent reports of mass exterminations of European Jews in Polish concentration camps began to reach the Allies, the Dutch government hardly responded, although the news was broadcast on the BBC on 26 June 1942 and one day later on Radio Orange, the voice of the Dutch government in exile.

Moshe Flinker had heard in Brussels in December 1942 that *a hundred thousand Jews were dying in the East*. He did not believe the downfall of the Third Reich would be the end of all the problems for the Jews. He was not convinced of the good intentions of the Allies; rather, he predicted an apocalyptic end with the *destruction of the largest part of the world, because everybody has tormented our people (...) It is as if everyone is laughing at our plight*.

When in the autumn of 1942 a representative of the Polish Resistance, Jan Karski, personally informed the British Minister of Foreign Affairs, Anthony Eden, and the American President Roosevelt about the gradual liquidation of the Warsaw Ghetto and about the extermination camp at Belzec, the US State Department and the British Foreign Office did not react to the requests for action against these proven Nazi atrocities. Typically perhaps, according to Karski the famous author H.G. Wells remarked, when he heard about the gruesome events that had taken place in the ghetto of Warsaw: *There is room for an important study, namely to establish what are the reasons that in every country where the Jews reside, sooner or later antisemitism emerges.*[18] Only Arthur Koestler delivered a talk on the BBC radio on behalf of Karski. The British and US governments seem to have decided that these reports should not be given too much publicity. The suicide in London of the Polish socialist leader Szmul Zygielbojm on 12 May 1943 hardly made it to the press. He had just received news that his wife and children had been deported from the Warsaw Ghetto, after the SS had smothered the uprising in blood and flames. *Perhaps my death will accomplish what my life could not: get something done.* But nothing was done. *It was beyond the belief and the comprehension of almost all people living at the time,* wrote De Jong, who himself worked for Radio Orange in London during the war.

In December 1943, a young lawyer, Bob Levisson, who had just escaped from Holland, informed the Dutch government in exile about *the systematic ... and complete liquidation of all Jews in the whole of the Netherlands.* It fell on deaf ears. Earlier, in September 1943, a Dutch underground newspaper used the term 'gas chamber' for the first time.

Yet, the information about the best-kept secret of the Second World War became more and more frequent, more and more detailed. In April 1944 two Czech Jews escaped from Birkenau. Based on their information, an urgent message was sent to Hungary, in order to warn the Hungarian Jews, who were about to be deported.[19] Via the papal nuncio in Czechoslovakia, the Vatican and the Western governments were informed about what was happening in Auschwitz-Birkenau. These were not the only prisoners who escaped, and they all did their utmost to be heard by the rest of the world. Churchill wrote in that same summer of 1944 to his Foreign Secretary Anthony Eden: *There is no doubt this is the most horrible crime ever committed in the whole history of the world, and it has been done by scientific machinery by nominally civilised men...*

Nevertheless, the world remained passive. This attitude on the part of the Allies was not only the result of incomprehension and indifference. Traditional antisemitism must also have played a significant part. Some people in the highest circles round Churchill and Roosevelt considered these reports 'Jewish propaganda'.[20]

Was there anything the Allies could have done? Etty Hillesum wondered on 24 August 1943 why the railway lines to the camps in Poland were not bombed, as she had earlier questioned why the Dutch underground did not blow up the line to Westerbork. Of course, to bomb railroads from the air was not always successful and German repairs would have been rapid. It is certain that the Allies could have bombed Auschwitz from 1944 on, when the airbases in Italy became available. The request was repeatedly made from the Jewish side, but in vain. The Allied Commanders and their political leaders did not consider it a priority. Everything had to be subordinate to that one goal: to defeat the Nazis. Allied bombers did appear above Birkenau, but only on their way to industrial targets.

The Jews were trapped between the reluctance of the Allies to help, the determination of the Nazis to murder them, and their own powerlessness, wrote the historian Yehuda Bauer.[21] The consequence for Durlacher and all the other inmates of Auschwitz, looking hopefully up at the sky, was one of utter despondency:

> The feeling that the world more or less discreetly turns the other way or watches unmoved while hundreds of thousands of people are systematically being killed all around you, and that you yourself know that every day you are still alive is a cruel trick of fate, is something that cannot adequately be expressed in words. (Durlacher, 1991:24)

Maybe Maurits Mok meant to express the very same delusion in a poem called *Under the Skin*:

> How high, how sky high
> above their dying despair
> the trees, the clouds, the stars remained silent.
> Seas cried unapproachably
> behind their final scream. No finger closed
> their extinguished eyes.

The End

Probably in early November 1944 Himmler ordered the suspension of all gassings in Auschwitz. He wanted to obliterate all traces of the destruction. As a result, the gas chambers and crematoriums were blown up, and the corpses were dug up from their mass graves to be burnt, usually by Jews who were put to death themselves immediately afterwards. Not a single shred of concrete evidence of one of the biggest genocides in world history was to be left behind.

In all the stories of those who were still alive by then, we hear of the terrible death marches. Elie Cohen was marched out of Auschwitz on 18 January 1945: *A miracle had happened: we left Auschwitz on our feet and not through the chimney, we were happy, we were marching as if we were going on holiday*. But the elation was short-lived:

> The road ahead was full of horror. Everywhere we walked past, we saw traces of the transports that had gone before us. Fearfully we looked at the corpses along the road: uncovered, with bashed-in skulls, with craniums shot away, with mutilated faces, sometimes no more than a pool of blood, men and women ... In the beginning we counted the corpses, but we lost count very soon. (Cohen, 1992:119, own translation)

Many people still died, so close to liberation, either through sheer exhaustion or through a bullet from an SS guard. Or we hear the stories, from

One of the grim scenes greeting the British Army when it entered Bergen-Belsen. The inmates simply did not have the strength left to give the dead a decent burial and just threw them out of the barracks

people like Renata Laqueur, about the ghostly train rides between the two fronts, in trains without food or water. She describes in her memoirs how she was liberated on 24 April – travelling in the same train as Abel Herzberg, Loden Vogel and Jaap Meijer and his family – by the Russian Red Army near the village of Tröbitz (between Leipzig and Dresden):

> I walked on and I saw a green uniform, a long coat, a rifle...and then...I saw the red star on his cap! It was true! I ran to him. I put my arms around him, I almost pulled off his hand from happiness. A Russian, a friend, the liberator from our misery! We had so much to say and we could not make ourselves understood. I laughed, he laughed... (Laqueur, 1965:142, own translation)

But even after liberation the hardship was not over yet; thousands would still lose their lives, in the hour of release, through disease (mainly typhus) and privation, or through eating – either too much or too quickly. Their stomachs could not manage the change.

Thus, the last days of the Third Reich were characterised by the same tragic pattern of murder, starvation, exposure and disease as had typified the whole brutal history of it.

Anne Frank: Auschwitz and Death in Bergen-Belsen

On the passenger list[22] of that last train from Westerbork to Auschwitz, departing 3 September 1944, the names of the four members of the Frank family appear as numbers 306 - 309. Otto Frank had still tried his utmost to make sure that his family was not sent to Auschwitz, but to Theresienstadt instead, believing that every day they could stay in Holland was a day nearer the end of the war, and that they perhaps had a better chance in that camp. The latter probably would have been an illusion, as the fate of the people on a later train to Theresienstadt – including virtually the whole Jewish Council and most of the cabaret-artistes of Westerbork – was to prove: most of those were taken to Auschwitz later. The journey took almost two days: in the night of 5/6 September, the train arrived in Auschwitz. The mood in the cattle truck had understandably been one of gloom. Janny Brandes-Brilleslijper was in the same car as the Franks, and the picture she gives is one of incredible tiredness: people had to stand all the time, because there was no room to sit or lie down. That caused a lot of irritation and aggression:

> The longer the trip lasted, the more belligerent people became. (...) The kindest, gentlest people become aggressive when they've stood for a long time. And you get tired – so terribly tired that you just want to lean against something, or if possible, even if only for a minute, to sit down on the straw. Then you sit on the straw, and they step on you from all sides because you are sitting so low. All those feet and all that noise around you make you aggressive (...) and then you, too, push and hit. (Lindwer, 1991:55)

The arrival at the station took place amid confusion and chaos: Auschwitz was very full after the arrival of the Hungarian Jews in August. Of the 1019 people on the transport from Westerbork, 549 were not registered in the camps administration, but taken to the gas chambers straightaway, among them all children under 15. Anne Frank, just over 15, her sister and mother escaped that fate; they were housed in the women's camp, where they had to try and survive the endless roll-calls, the frequent selections, the starvation diet, the bitter cold of the nights. Hygiene and sanitary conditions were abominable, so the risk of infection was considerable. Anne Frank developed scabies and had to be taken to the Krätzeblock (the quarantine barrack for people with infectious skin diseases). One of the women from her barrack tells how her sister Margot went to stay with her there, much to the despair of their mother:

She didnt even eat the piece of bread that she got. Together with her I dug up a hole under the wooden wall of the barracks where the children were. The ground was rather soft and so you could dig a hole if you had strength, and I did. Mrs. Frank stood next to me and just asked, "Is it working? "Yes," I answered. I dug close in under the wood, and through the hole we could speak with the girls. Margot took that piece of bread that I pushed through underneath, and they shared that. (Lindwer, 1991:155)

Ronnie Goldstein-van Cleef was also in the Krätzeblock at that time; she remembers how she and the others had to get through the ordeal of seeing other people die of typhus and other diseases. Those people were just left and would lie there for days, before they were dragged away. For her, that seems to have been the worst:

That is something which is more than loathsome – those dead women lying there for days, until they came and threw them into the carts. The carts which were actually intended for emptying the latrines. They were used to pick up bodies everywhere, and the bodies were just thrown, hup, on top of each other. I always thought that was so dreadful. Actually, I didnt want to see it at all, but I still had to look. I was compelled to look – that was terrible. (...) The Frank girls saw it, too. And they experienced precisely what I experienced. (...) The emotional shock at the existence of something like that – they felt that as well. (Lindwer, 1991:190)

Anne and Margot Frank would not stay long in Auschwitz. With the Russian armies coming closer every day, the Germans wanted the camp evacuated and began to send inmates from Auschwitz – the biggest camp – to other camps. Towards the end of 1944, the haste to empty out Auschwitz would result in the frightful so-called death marches – long columns of walking skeletons, marching through the snow until they dropped – but in October people were still sent all over Germany by train. Presumably on 28 October 1944, the two girls were taken to Bergen-Belsen, together with many other girls and women who still looked relatively fit and strong. Their mother, Edith, was left behind in Auschwitz; she died there of exhaustion in the beginning of January 1945. People in Bergen-Belsen were not murdered deliberately and systematically, but under the circumstances that difference was of very little significance. Because of massive overpopulation, lack of food, proper clothing, inadequate hygiene, collapsing medical care and a harsh winter, people died on the same scale as in the actual death camps. As the whole of Germany was collapsing, the suffering of the inmates of the concentration camp only seemed to increase. The transfer from Auschwitz to Bergen-Belsen was therefore not a good one for Anne Frank. Janny Brandes-Brilleslijper writes about the first night in Bergen-Belsen:

Large tents were put up hastily because, as we heard later, Bergen-Belsen had not counted on these transports at all. Beds were shoved into those army tents, one, two, three on top of each other. We were soaked and cold, and as soon as the tents were up, everyone ran to them.(...) During the night there was a terrible storm, with thunder and lightning and hail and you name it (...). Two or three tents, including ours, collapsed. In each tent, there were a couple of hundred people. A lot of people were injured and, I think, even a few died.(...) There was terrible devastation. And in the morning, it was as if there had been a shipwreck. People and piles of wreckage everywhere – moaning and pain. (Lindwer, 1991:67)

That was only the beginning: the winter of 1944/45 would turn out to be one of the severest ones of this century. To stay warm became a major undertaking for these underfed and underclad people. To go around undressed under those circumstances indicates a level of despair that is hard to imagine in these days of central heating and an abundance of food. Yet Anne's revulsion and horror of the fleas and the lice in her clothes had driven her to throw all her clothes away. She went through the camp with only one blanket wrapped around her. Her friend from primary schooldays, Hannah Goslar, quite unexpectedly ran into Anne in Bergen-Belsen. Hannah had landed in the privileged part of the camp – which was by now in quite a state itself – and one evening she was told that her friend Anne Frank was in the other part of the camp. She went to look for her through the barbed wire and finally found her. It was an emotional meeting:

It wasn't the same Anne. She was a broken girl. I probably was, too, but it was so terrible. She immediately began to cry, and she told me, "I don't have any parents anymore." I remember that with absolute certainty. That was terribly sad, because she couldn't have known anything else.(...) I always think if Anne had known that her father was still alive, she might have had more strength to survive. (Lindwer, 1991:27/28)

After this first meeting Hannah promised to do what she could to get some clothes and food for her. The first time she threw a small parcel over the fence, Anne did not see it coming – she was very shortsighted – and somebody else caught it and refused to give it to her. The second time Anne caught it, but it was the last time the two friends saw each other, because soon afterwards Anne got sick and Hannah's father died. It is estimated that by the end of that winter, more than half of the roughly 200,000 inmates of Bergen-Belsen were suffering from typhus or some other contagious infection like dysentery. Most of those died between February and April 1945, and many still died after the camp was liberated on 15 April by the British Army. The Frank sisters also got sick. First, Margot died of typhus, then one or two days later Anne died as well. An eyewitness from the same barrack recalls:

The Frank girls were so emaciated. They looked terrible. They had little squabbles, caused by their illness, because it was clear that they had typhus (...) They had those hollowed-out faces, skin over bone. They were terribly cold.(...) You could really see both of them dying. (...) They showed the recognizable symptoms of typhus – that gradual wasting away, a sort of apathy, with occasional revivals, until they became so sick that there wasn't any hope. (Lindwer, 1991:104)

This eyewitness, Rachel van Amerongen-Frankfoorder, has more sobering tales to tell, among others about the way people who had died during the night were disposed of. Usually, they were unceremoniously thrown out of the barrack by the survivors, after these had appropriated their clothes and blankets:

The dead were always carried outside, laid down in front of the barracks, and when you were let out in the morning to go to the latrine, you had to walk past them. That was just as dreadful as going to the latrine itself, because gradually everyone got typhus. In front of the barracks was a kind of wheelbarrow in which you could take care of your needs. Sometimes you also had to take those wheelbarrows to the latrine. Possibly it was on one of those trips to the latrine that I walked past the bodies of the Frank sisters, one or both – I don't know. At the time, I assumed that the bodies of the Frank girls had also been put down in front of the barracks. And then the heaps would be cleared away. A huge hole would be dug and they were thrown into it. That I'm sure of. That must have been their fate, because that's what happened with other people. I don't have a single reason for assuming that it was any different for them than for the other women with us who died at the same time. (Lindwer, 1991:104)

From that last transport of 1019 people from Westerbork to Auschwitz, 45 men and 82 women survived the war.

Anne Frank as the world knows her. Few are willing to picture her last months

VI
The Paradox of Silence: Survivors and Losers

"You know, Ben," she said musing, "what amazes me most is our memory, how it works. Why you forget one thing and remember another." (Minco, 1990:50)

Above all I charge the leaders of the nation and those under them to scrupulous observance of the laws of race and to merciless opposition to the universal poisoner of all peoples, international Jewry. (from Hitler's testament)

On 30 April 1945, Adolf Hitler committed suicide in the Führerbunker in Berlin, together with the woman he had married one day earlier, Eva Braun. On 8 May 1945, the German Army capitulated officially.

In Holland the German forces had capitulated two days earlier, although the southern part of the country had already been liberated in the autumn of 1944. The liberators, mainly Canadian, English and American troops, had been received enthusiastically by the Dutch population wherever they went. Among those Dutch people was the almost 5-year-old Jewish boy Robert Krell, who had survived in hiding for three years. His liberation carried some dark undertones with it:

Liberation was not particularly liberating, for within a few days I was 'liberated' from those I loved (...) to rejoin my father and mother who had emerged from their respective hiding places. I cried in protest, and they had to prove I was theirs with photos taken when I was aged about one and a half. Of course, I was actually the luckiest of all children in having my parents survive. Try telling that to a 5 year old with no memory of them, after nearly three years with another family. (Gilbert, 1995:73-75)

It was a reunion that was indicative of the trouble that lay ahead. Cornelia T. had also survived the war in hiding. Her family had been deported to Sobibor. She would write later:

Came the 5th of May 1945, and at last the war was over – my reaction on that day: why were they (the public) singing and dancing in the street. Indeed, the war was over, but I lost my entire family. I was devastated. (Gilbert, 1995:78)

Cornelia spoke for many, although not many paid much attention during those exciting days of May 1945. A few, however, realised that the worst was still to come. The haberdasher from Zandvoort, Ies Dikker, wrote during the final months of the occupation:

> Now we can expect the liberation any day, we know that from Holland alone more than 100,000 Jews have been deported; we have to assume that only a few of them will still be alive. (Dikker: 1995:41, own translation)

Dikker was right: of the 107,000 Jews deported from Holland, only 5200 would return. Compared with other countries this was relatively and absolutely the highest number of murdered Jews in the whole of Western Europe. How was that possible? A question that has been asked with ever increasing urgency during the past 50 years. Fifty years after liberation, in a speech before the Israeli Knesset, Queen Beatrix undermined the image that the Dutch had helped the Jews on a massive scale. Holland was not only the country where Anne Frank could go into hiding, but also the country where she was betrayed:

> We know that many of our fellow-countrymen put up courageous – and some-times successful – resistance, and often, exposing themselves to mortal danger, stood by their threatened fellow men...But we also know that they were the exceptional ones and that the people of the Netherlands could not prevent the destruction of their Jewish fellow-citizens. (Knesset Speech, March 28, 1995)

This speech reflects the spirit of a book written during the last year of the war, *Verduisterde jaren* (Darkened Years), by S. de Vries Jr. In a book that was *not* written with the knowledge that the majority of the Dutch Jewry had perished, one reads:

> There are too many Dutchmen who know much, but do nothing. There are too many who profess to adhere to tough opposition with their mouths, but have already consented to soft cooperation in their actions. There are too many who were and are prepared to fill the open places, the places of deported Jews or of men who fell in true resistance. (De Vries, 1945:331, own translation)

*

After the liberation an atmosphere of desperate thrill-seeking grew in non-Jewish intellectual and artistic circles, comparable with the 'années folles' in the nightclubs of existentialist Paris where authors like Jean-Paul Sartre and Simone de Beauvoir enjoyed performances of Boris Vian and Juliette Gréco. The difference was that in Holland it was at times mixed with a deep sense of guilt: how was it possible that the country had allowed 107,000 Jews to be deported from under their noses? And the consequences were visible. One small example was the cultural life in Amsterdam, which had become unrecognizable to anybody who had known it before the war. After the occupation there were only 25,000 Jews left, 10,000 of them in

Saved! But who saves her from her memories?

Amsterdam; the city would never appear the same again. All the more so because the decimation of Dutch Jewry had hit hardest among the proletariat: street vendors and stallholders had disappeared forever. They had not had the money or the contacts to go into hiding.

A deep cut had been made into Dutch society, a psychological wound that certainly was not healed with liberation. That became clear almost immediately when survivors began to return from the camps.

The Liberation of the Camps

As stated above, of the 107,000 deported Jews, no more than 5200 returned from the camps: 1150 came from Auschwitz, 19 from Sobibor, 2000 from Bergen-Belsen, 1500 from Theresienstadt, and a few hundred from Ravensbrück and other camps. Some would only arrive in Holland after a long odyssey. How did they feel about it?

Greet van Amstel (1903-1981), an artist who became involved in the Dutch resistance, was liberated in Auschwitz. On her way back she put her mixed feelings about her liberation into words on the beach of Odessa[1]:

> When I lie here on the warm sand and I gaze into the blue space of sea and air, I sometimes get such a sinking feeling, and all my thoughts seem empty; there is only place for an indescribable sorrow. I would like to cry, but I can't. The others also tell me confidentially they are often overwhelmed by a feeling of grief and bitterness. The past has been burned away and thinking about the future fills us with despair and fear.
>   We will never really 'return', we will never really be among the 'others' again. The shadows of the camp will be with us forever. Death, whom we knew to be near all the time, the smoke, the barbaric dehumanization that we have seen and experienced will doom all our efforts to rejoin the others and live a normal life again to failure. (Van Amstel, 1965:64, own translation)

This calls to mind the title of the book by the French Auschwitz survivor Charlotte Delbo *Aucun de nous ne reviendra* (None of Us Will Return), which also suggests that the people who have gone through experiences like the death camps leave part of their old selves behind and, in a sense, never do come back.

In *The Respite*, Primo Levi has most penetratingly described the feelings of shame and diffidence in the liberators of the camps when they were confronted with *evil committed by others, because now it exists, now it is irrevocably part of the world of existing things, whereas his good will had been worthless and insufficient and couldn't prevent it.*

The British troops that liberated Bergen-Belsen were so stunned and shocked at what they saw – those emaciated survivors, those heaps of corpses – that they collected the inhabitants of all the neighbouring villages and made them come and see what had been perpetrated in their name. Afterwards, the burning of the barracks, the digging of huge mass graves, the shoving by bulldozers of mountains of corpses into the freshly dug graves – all was accurately filmed by Hitchcock and his crew. The Western Allies passed the horrible images of the camps that they had liberated almost immediately on to the public, although the BBC withheld Richard Dimbleby's radio broadcast about the camps for three days on the grounds of disbelief. All the more remarkable is the fact that what had happened in the Polish camps remained unknown for a long time. In the first Soviet report on Nazi atrocities, the names of Auschwitz and Birkenau were not even mentioned, nor were the Jews mentioned as the main victims. Only in the Sixties after the Eichmann and other trials would Auschwitz become the symbol for the Holocaust that it is today.

Many American soldiers had never really understood what the war in Europe was all about, but when they entered their first concentration camp and saw the starved survivors, one of them wrote: *Now I know why I am here.*

Some American soldiers, however, did not feel much sympathy for the Jews, even after seeing the camps. General George S. Patton, for instance, called the Jews he encountered in Bavaria *a sub-human species without any of the cultural or social refinements of our time*. Sometimes this lack of understanding even grew when observing the behaviour of survivors, which was incomprehensible in the eyes of the liberators and even 'egotistical': they could not understand the sole interest in food and a continuing desire to steal it, even when there was enough to eat. The 200,000 Jewish survivors in the Allied Displaced Persons Camps in Germany were often treated with little respect. After a couple of months, President Truman had to step in personally to bring about some improvements.

This lack of understanding was to a great extent caused by the unimaginable character of the Shoah. *Archeologists in a modern ruin*, Robert Abzug called the American journalists who visited Natzweiler concentration camp and had difficulty believing their own eyes: a *'so-called lethal gas chamber'*, *'stains which appeared to be caused by blood'* are examples of a stylistic effort to keep one's sanity intact.

The Conspiracy of Silence

The return to Holland that many had achieved on foot or by hitch-hiking and only after much hardship was a bitter disillusion. Help with repatriation came more slowly for the Dutch men and women in the concentration camps than for other nationals from Western European countries. The Dutch Red Cross and the Dutch government were conspicuous by their absence, even after Germany was defeated. Durlacher and others mention that the receptions were badly organised and compared unfavourably with those in France and Belgium. The explanation can be paradoxically explained by the refusal, in itself praiseworthy, of the Dutch Government to recognize the difference the Germans had made between Jews and non-Jews. Even during the war the government had decreed that Jews *were Dutchmen like all other Dutchmen* and would therefore not be treated differently. Good intentions, however, can all too easily have the opposite result if executed bureaucratically, as in this case where it led to a refusal to acknowledge the serious nature of the Jewish experiences during the war. German Jews in particular were hard hit; having come to Holland in the Thirties as political refugees, they were still treated as Germans by the Dutch administration, i.e. as enemy aliens. They did not qualify for any assistance. A large percentage of them emigrated to Palestine for this very reason.

The frosty bureaucratic treatment by the authorities would sometimes subject the camp survivors to endless interrogations, and on occasion they would be locked up in one cell with Dutch Nazis or Nazi collaborators. The

Jews returned to Holland find time to write a little note to family who in too many cases would not be there

same camps – Vught, Westerbork – would often be used to house these collaborators and, in a number of cases, repatriated Jews.

Even more hurtful was the behaviour of those whom one had once believed to be trustworthy. The author Andreas Burnier wrote about her feelings of alienation after having spent years in hiding. She returned to relatives who had survived the camps:

> None of us could bear being with the others. Like all survivors we had suffered; those coming back from the east the most. But all, the children, the adults, the elderly, we had all looked into the abyss of death by terror. We had been immensely lost and lonely. Now we needed years of comfort: an endlessly loving and caring mother goddess, through whom we would be reborn, who would undo history. But who could that have been? They who had the age of mothers and grandmothers, of fathers and grandfathers had suffered the most. We, the young, still had the harness of our youth, be it battered and broken. (Burnier, 1995: 134/135; own translation)

Gerard Durlacher, having lost both his parents, was among the first in Holland to research experiences of returnees. Astonished and with barely contained jealousy, he quotes Primo Levi, who returned to Turin after a journey of nine months and wrote in *The Truce* about *the liberating joy of recounting my story.* Durlacher had different experiences himself when he came back in the summer of 1945:

> My house was still standing. The occupants, recipients of privileges from the occupying powers in 1943, did not allow me to cross the threshold. My parents and the other residents of our house were 'missing'(...) A few family members who no longer expected me turned up. Highly principled friends of my parents and neighbours, some decent and some not, each had their story of the hardships of the occupation, which made me choke back the unspeakable. I was the near stranger who had to listen to everything that everyone else had heard over and over again, and I bought acceptance with my willing ear and discrete silence. (Durlacher, 1991:100).

Renata Laqueur, who was liberated by the Russian army together with many other survivors of Bergen-Belsen near Tröbitz, described her reluctance to talk about her camp experiences in 1946:

> We heard about Holland, about executions, hunger, strikes, liberation. We didn't know a thing. We had to tell our story, but we couldn't yet.[2] (Laqueur, 1965: 152)

All their stories met with disbelief and incomprehension. Camp survivors had to listen to long stories about the hunger winter of 1944/1945 or about German atrocities: *Do you know what happened to me? Germans stole my bicycle...*Incomprehension and, worse, denial made it painfully clear to the returned Jews that they could not take their presence in Holland after liberation for granted. This incomprehension was often experienced as antisemitism, even if not meant as such. Having returned from the camps, Jews were often blamed for not having been in Holland. Therefore, they could not participate in the collective memory of the rest of the nation like German reprisals, Allied bombings, forced labour camps in Germany, the 'hunger winter', events that had left the deepest impression by far on the memory of most Dutch people. Interest in the experiences of other groups was minimal, as later people returning from the Japanese prisoner-of-war camps were to discover as well.

Non-Jewish Dutch people responded unbelievingly when they saw the photos – in the summer of 1945 – of mass graves in Bergen-Belsen and other camps in their newspapers. Feelings of guilt about the passive attitude of most were sometimes translated into increased antisemitism – the returnees being the living proof of their failure – or philosemitism.

In a certain sense, one can therefore maintain that the Nazis did win the war in one way: the separation they had so systematically made between Jews and non-Jews had stuck. Consciously or unconsciously, the Dutch had been taught to think in terms of Jewish, non-Jewish, half-Jewish and Aryan.

'Friends' who had been entrusted with house and possessions now claimed never to have known those who returned. Those Dutch people who refused

to hand back to the survivors goods that had been entrusted to them by
Jewish friends or neighbours were called 'bewariërs'.[3] In some cases it took
court cases lasting many years before one's possessions were handed back.

Old habits were dying hard: the Receiver of Revenue used a form with
a big J until 1951. Insurance companies cancelled policies because survivors
had not paid their premiums while in hiding or in the camps, new marriages were impossible without formal proof that the former partner had
died. For years one could be involved in such procedures of rehabilitation.

For many, these post-war years were almost as traumatizing as the years
of the war themselves. Some Jewish women were called 'Jerry whores' after
their return from the camps, because they had hardly any hair on their head
(this refers to the practice after liberation of shaving the heads of girlfriends
of German soldiers). Even more serious were some expressions of public
antisemitism. One survivor was told in a crowded tram: *Bloody Jewess, they
have forgotten to gas you as well.*

When the poet and painter Greet van Amstel returned to Holland from
Auschwitz, she heard someone say: *Careful, don't come too close, they probably
have lice.* Her husband and two of her children had been murdered by the
Germans. All her pre-war work had been destroyed by the Nazis. Her
poem, *There was no Darkness on the Earth*, begins with a dedication to her
deceased husband and children and continues:

> the world has long perished
> we know:
> life is possible no longer.
> the heart is gone,
> destroyed.
> only the hearts of those who died pointlessly
> live forever.
> in us.
> around us.
> but the earth
> and the sky are empty.
> over everything
> always
> the red shadow of grief. (Van Amstel, 1965:5, own translation)

And she wrote these bitter lines about life after her return:

> We are doomed to live
> between fungi of misunderstanding
> and needles of hate (Van Amstel, 1965:76, own translation)

Repeatedly, Jews were advised in the daily press to remain as invisible as
possible in order to avoid antisemitism. As Presser remarked sarcastically:
amid the ruins, *we had to act normal again.* On the whole, these outbursts of

antisemitism did not last long. The majority of the Dutch people just wanted to forget and get on with rebuilding the devastated country.

It was a difficult post-war period of reconstruction and recovery. War damage was substantial, and it is not surprising that material everyday problems were of great concern to every Dutch person. Internationally, attention was focussed on issues like decolonization, fear of communism, the Cold War. Holland unexpectedly became part of that worldwide conflict over the granting of independence to Indonesia. At first, the Dutch were unwilling even to think about secession. After two military actions to try and still the rebellion, independence had to be granted to the Republic of Indonesia in 1949 after heavy international pressure, in particular, from the USA. Many considered this a humiliation and a betrayal; the consensus was that the episode should be forgotten as soon as possible.

It was repressed so quickly that it resurfaces regularly. Holland became familiar with the traumas of decolonization and still feels the effects after 50 years. A tendency to repress the disagreeable side of this development was linked with the more unsavoury aspects of Holland's recent war history. This can be explained as a consequence of hurt national pride over the humiliating military defeats against Germany and Japan, the loss of Indonesia and the fate of the Dutch Jews.

Comfort was only found in the knowledge of a heroic Dutch resistance. Soon after the war, the myth of a truly national resistance developed, which had, it was assumed, contributed considerably to the Allied victory. The heroism of ordinary citizens, united in their refusal to obey an alien doctrine – that is what had to be remembered; the rest was silence, repression and forgetting.

To a certain extent, this might help to explain the fanaticism with which the conflict surrounding Jewish war foster children was fought out. Almost 4500 Jewish children had been in hiding with foster parents during the German occupation. After the war about 3500 of them resurfaced. Almost half of them were reunited with one or both parents, more than 2000 were not. The question arose to whom those 2000 children belonged. 'In the interest of the Jewish child',[4] many orphans did not return to a Jewish sphere of life, but stayed with their Christian foster parents. Fear of antisemitism was cited as an important argument for leaving orphans with their non-Jewish foster parents and letting them assimilate. Being Jewish was considered by many a burden one could do without. Two girls, awarded to the custody of Jewish families because of their murdered parents' orthodox background, were even kidnapped and taken out of the country by the former foster parents. Even 50 years later, many of these children suffer serious problems of identity.

The problem was particularly pertinent where Jewish orphans ended up in new families. Bronia Davidson, who came back to Amsterdam after long wanderings via Samarkand and Lodz, described the atmosphere at school:

In class Death had taken its seat next to every child. A few children had two parents, like Anna, a spirited girl, who not only had parents, but a little brother as well. My friend Sara, with an even thicker braid than myself, lived with a stepmotherly aunt. All replacement mothers were evil stepmothers, who couldn't match the beautiful memory of the mother we sometimes hardly had known. How faithful we were to those buried, gassed, executed parents. (Davidson, 1995: 116-117, own translation)

Jona Oberski, who had lost both his parents, dedicated his book *Childhood* to his foster parents, *who had quite a time with me*. He ends by telling how difficult it was to adjust to his new life with his foster parents:

She (the foster mother) pulled my head toward her and kissed me on the lips. My legs trembled. My hands grabbed the plate and threw it on the floor. I stamped on it, I burst out crying and I screamed: "You kissed me on the lips. Now I'll die. My mother told me herself." My mouth filled with vomit. I almost suffocated. It came splashing out on the floor. It spattered her legs. She said: "Now look what you've done. Just clean it up. You're not a baby any more." She gave me a cloth. I started wiping it up.[5] (Oberski, 1984: 123)

Where one or both parents had survived, they often had to put up not only with the frosty reception of their own home-coming, but also with disappointments about their children, idealised during the years in the camps, who had become attached to their Christian foster parents. The Dutch writer Judith Herzberg, daughter of Abel Herzberg, had been hidden by a Dutch family while her parents were taken to a concentration camp. In one of her poems, she recalls how she rejoined her mother, who had become a stranger:

Reunion

For years I had not seen such a town
or stood at the bottom of such stairs
as on that hot day, in black Sunday best
and leather shoes. And at the top
I saw vaguely my strange mother
I'd have to give her a kiss.

Soft cuddling that night after night
I'd pretended, to creep from
the war into sleep,
was dividing us now. Too grown-up,
too skinny and countrified, I took
it all back. Was this
really my mother?

Come up, she said,
winking to put me at ease,
but with both eyes at once.
Right then I thought we should say
the goodbyes we'd delayed,
but I didn't know how to look at her
with my difficult eyes. (Herzberg, 1988:34)

For a long time, many people were unsure about the fate of their deported family members. In the absence of news, they kept hoping against all odds for their return.

For years after 1945, many went to the stations to wait for the trains from Eastern Europe. In the last chapter of *Bitter Herbs*, Marga Minco describes a visit to her uncle, her father's brother:

Some weeks after the Liberation I visited my uncle at Zeist. The Germans had left him alone because he was married to a Gentile woman. Although I had not written to him beforehand, he was standing at the tram stop. "How did you know I was coming?" I asked him. "I wait at the stop every day," he said. "I look to see whether your father's coming." "But you've had the news from the Red Cross too, haven't you?" "Yes," he said. "They can say all that; but I don't believe it. You never can tell, can you?"

At the end of the visit, she gets up; her uncle offers to take her to the tram stop:

"I'll walk along with you," he said, looking at his watch. "The tram'll be here any minute." But the tram was already there and on the point of leaving. I said good-bye in a hurry and jumped in. As we drove off, I waved to him from the rear balcony. But he did not wave back. He was looking at the tram approaching from the other direction, from Utrecht, and I realized that he had meant that one. Before we turned the corner I saw him, a small, bowed figure, scrutinizing the travellers who got out at the stop. (Minco, 1960:111-114)

A majority of the Jews felt completely isolated, cut off from the rest of society, thrown back upon themselves. Reactions varied. *Even though they knew they were not guilty, it didn't change the fact that others expected them to feel guilty*, Bruno Bettelheim, himself a survivor of the camps and after the war a famous psychoanalyst in New York, wrote. Some changed their religion, others became orthodox. Many left Holland, the place where they did not know anybody any longer and where they were confronted with so many sad memories. Marga Minco tells about one of the protagonists in her novel, *The Fall*:

After his liberation from the camp, he and other typhus patients had been nursed in a hospital in the south. Two pieces of news reached him which caused him to

leave the country: he alone of his family had survived the war, and the belongings from his parents' house had vanished. He signed on with a freighter, and
after a number of trips he remained in the United States. There he had gone
through a hundred jobs, been married and divorced, been poverty-stricken and
fairly well off, and had ended up driving a truck with which he criss-crossed the
northern states for so long that he could no longer bear to see a highway. Urged
by a friend, he went with him to Brazil, thought that he had finally found peace
in an organization run by Dutch farmers. But when, during a yearly market in
the neighbouring town, he recognized one of his camp guards – 'Der Knuppel',
'the Club' – among the rancheros, he decided that the time had come to take an
aeroplane back. (Minco, 1990:48-49)

It was difficult to find a house: Holland was (and still is) an overpopulated
country in dire need of housing. In the first eight years after the war, at least
5000 Jews emigrated, mainly to the USA and after 1948 to Israel. After the
Six-Day War of 1967, there was a second wave of immigrants to Israel.

*

Did the returnees have feelings of revenge towards their persecutors?
Durlacher writes that he learnt from newspaper reports on 2 October 1945
about the death sentences of prominent Nazis in Nuremberg, among whom
was Seyss-Inquart.[6] He ends with: *I am grateful to the judges, but I fear that
their verdict will not release us from the nightmares and the sorrow.*

After the war, 36 war criminals were executed in Holland, among them
not only German Nazis and Dutch collaborators, but also the Jewish
woman Ans van Dijk, found guilty of betraying more than 100 Jews. The
two chairmen of the Jewish Council, Asscher and Cohen, were found guilty
of 'reprehensible behaviour' by a special Jewish Court of Honour. Both
were excluded for life from holding official functions within the Jewish
community.

The Jews were an injured group in an injured society. Survivors of the
camps were badly equipped for a return to society. They had to live harder
and more fiercely than people with normal histories. Many youngsters
returned without skills or education. Even more serious were the psychological wounds: survivors found it impossible to use ordinary words like
'fetch', 'send through', 'transport', 'selection'. Of this conspiracy of silence,
Marga Minco gives an example in *The Fall*, one of her novels in which the
words 'Jew' or 'Jewish' do not occur:

When (...) she found him with his sleeves rolled up busy unplugging her sink,
she spotted the number on his arm. "Let me see," she said. It slipped out before
she knew. Timidly he turned his arm towards her. She cast a cursory glance at
it and immediately looked away, whereupon he quickly rolled down his sleeve.
There were those who had let it be removed, but sailors are used to tattoos, she
realized. Not until a few years later (...) had she asked him that absurd question:

whether he had perhaps encountered one of the others over there. He had merely shaken his head. After that they had never again spoken about that period. (Minco, 1990:50-51)

After the Shoah it had become impossible to speak freely about being Jewish. The uninhibitedness of before the war had disappeared.

As we saw earlier, during the first few years after 1945, Holland experienced an upsurge of antisemitism. On the other hand, feelings of guilt sometimes led to an exaggerated love of Jews. Thus, Holland became Israel's most loyal ally in the West, after its foundation in 1948. The survivors of the camps felt that the physical integrity of Jewish life was somehow connected to the continued existence of Israel, and they felt physically threatened in their existence every time Israel had to fight for its survival.

Durlacher writes that he could only rent a holiday cottage in Drente, not too far from concentration camp Westerbork, many years after the war:

The Six Day War in the Middle East destroyed our pastoral idyll. With a small transistor radio held to my ear, I followed the conflict. My heart pounding with fear, I listened to the sombre reports and I feared that Israel, the last refuge in times of persecutions, would perish. Suddenly I felt constricted in the guilty landscape of Drente, through which every Tuesday morning for three long years an endless chain of brick-red cattletrucks had driven, on board each train a cargo of one thousand Jews doomed to die. (Durlacher, 1993:33-34, own translation)

Jewish identity in Holland is, more than in other countries, determined by the existence of the State of Israel. Loyalty to that country has not led to a significant increase in the number of Zionists, but found expression in financial support and frequent official visits to Israel. Although the number of critics in Holland increased after the war of 1967, the Dutch population has generally remained supportive of Israel, an attitude that doubtlessly had much to do with the Shoah and the feeling that this time one wanted to behave better than during the Second World War.

Among non-Jews, an increased interest had grown for what had happened to the Jews during the war. What De Jong called the 'immense suppression', a 'collective locking up', came to an end in the Sixties. One of the first catalysts in this process of consciousness-raising was the trial against the mastermind behind the organization of the *Endlösung*, Adolf Eichmann, who had been abducted from Argentina by the Israeli Secret Service and taken to Israel. There he was to stand trial in 1961 and be held accountable for his deeds in the presence of the whole world: it was the first trial to be seen on television. The report of the trial by the German-American philosopher Hannah Arendt, *Eichmann in Jerusalem: The Banality of Evil*, made a deep impression in Holland. Abel Herzberg also witnessed the proceedings. He wrote: *Eichmann is a human being and, I fear, quite an ordinary*

human being at that. He lives among us everywhere in the world. He is like us.
(Herzberg, 1962:189, own translation)

Novelist Harry Mulisch, who also attended the trial, went one step further in *De zaak 40/61*. He wrote that Eichmann was nothing but a machine, without a will of his own, doing nothing but obeying orders. Mulisch believed Eichmann when he emphatically stated that he did not hate Jews and that he was no antisemite. For Herzberg, however, belief in a racial ideology is typical for perpetrators like Eichmann.

Four years later – in 1965 – Presser's *Ondergang* (Ashes in the Wind) went from reprint to reprint, although historical bestsellers were (and are) rarities in Holland. The reader was faced in many cases for the very first time with eyewitness accounts of survivors. Through *Ondergang* they learnt exactly what happened with the Jews in the war. Jews had been integrated into Dutch society more than anywhere else; more than anywhere else they had consequently been deserted.

Presser had felt capable of writing this study only after he had first published *The Night of the Girondists* in 1957 and he had felt 'cured'. The cure was not entirely successful, however, because he would later remark that he had written *Ondergang* 'with blood', after doing research for 15 years on it. He had completely identified with the victims, and it was noticeable in his very personal, emotional style. It can be read as an effort to redeem his own guilt towards the victims.[7]

Another explanation for the success of the book is that in the middle of the Sixties, the time was right. It was the right time for the exposure of a society that had been so well-organized and so law-abiding that it had cost the Germans little trouble to execute the deportations. During the Sixties a generation gap came to light: just as abroad – Berkeley, Paris – youth movements protested against the 'establishment'. The older generation was 'de-mythologized', a generation that had not behaved as heroically as it had wanted to believe. The protests against the war in Vietnam were compared by a younger generation with the resistance against the Germans. The younger succeeded where the older had failed.

In this atmosphere of rebelliousness and revolt against authority, the Weinreb affair broke. Friedrich Weinreb, originally from Eastern Europe, had played a complex double-game during the war, seemingly helping Jews, but at the same time working for the Gestapo. After the war he was found guilty by a Dutch court. According to those people who wanted to rehabilitate him, he was the victim of a judicial error, because he had to serve as a scapegoat for the failure of so many others. His memoirs, significantly called *Collaboratie en Verzet* (Collaboration and Resistance), made a deep impression on the generation of the Sixties, who considered him a hero who had opposed the 'establishment' of his time. That generation, brought up in the belief of the resistance myth, began to believe that collaboration had been widespread. Later, it was established that Weinreb was a fraud, whose memoirs could not be trusted.

One's behaviour during the war, however, remained the moral touch-stone on which politicians and public figures would be judged in the future. The sentences against war criminals continued to excite public opinion until far into the Eighties: the activities of Nazi hunter Simon Wiesenthal were especially followed with admiration. The Dutch novelist Harry Mulisch, one of the many Dutch writers fascinated by the Second World War, describes in *The Assault* the response of an ex-resistance fighter after the Dutch government decided in 1966 to release one of the last four German war criminals, Willy Lages:[8]

> 'Because he's sick, our dear little Willy. You'll see how soon he recovers back in Germany. And yet he made a lot of people really sick – but that's not so important. All those humane do-gooders with their respect for human life at our expense. The war criminal is sick, oh dear, the poor lamb. Free the Fascist quickly, for we're no Fascists, our hands are clean. Does this make his victims ill? What a hateful lot, those anti-Fascists – they're no better themselves! That's what they'll say next, you'll see. And who'll be the first to approve of this release? All those who kept their hands clean during the war – Catholics in the lead, of course. It's not for nothing that he converted to Catholicism the minute he went to prison. But if he gets to heaven, then I prefer hell...' (Mulisch, 1986:149)

It was not until 1989 that the remaining two German war criminals in Holland were released, amid much highly emotional protest of numerous war victims. One of them was Hauptsturmführer Aus der Fünten whom we have seen in action on many occasions.

*

Also in literature, newspapers, monuments, TV films and documentaries the war lives on, and since the Seventies, more than ever. At the end of that decade the American TV serial *Holocaust* drew much attention, as did feature films like *Sophie's Choice* and *Schindler's List*. It seems as if face to face with the Holocaust, the traditional difference between documentaries and feature films loses its relevance, as witnessed by the popular acclaim of *Shoah*, by French film-maker Claude Lanzmann. This film, lasting more than nine hours, consists mainly of testimonies from survivors, perpetrators and bystanders. A new genre emerged concerning the Jewish victims: the camp documentary. The suffering of the individual human being became the focus of emotional searches. Gerard Durlacher, for instance, looked in America and Israel for other survivors of his work detail in Auschwitz,[9] and Willy Lindwer did the same concerning the last months of Anne Frank. Personal histories are connected by images of rails, 'guilty landscapes' and testimonies of perpetrators and sheepish bystanders. The actual events seem to lose interest in favour of the moral choices people faced in those days and the individual suffering that was experienced.

The Victims

As mentioned before, after the war some 25,000 Jews were left in Holland. Many Jews refused to register out of 'registration fear'. Involvement in Jewish religious life shrank more and more, until it included no more than 25% of all Jews. Many had lost their religion altogether. They could not accept or believe that God would let his 'own' people suffer like this. It was inconceivable to them that those who betrayed the Jewish religion by having themselves baptized or by marrying out of the faith were saved, whereas the ones who remained true to their God were destroyed. Physician Elie Cohen wrote: *My answer to the question 'what about my trust in God after the war?' has developed into: 'I have left God in Auschwitz'. I really regret this, God has left me, and nothing has taken his place.* (Cohen, 1992:92)

Only the older generation tended to remember how much talent had been crushed by Hitler. In a number of books published after the war by Jewish authors, there is a recognizable mood of nostalgia, for example in the *Memorbook* by Mozes Gans (quoted in chapter I) and in books and poems where authors like Jaap Meijer and Maurits Mok recreate the world of prewar Jewry. The small Jewish generation that had survived the war began searching for the lives of those who had been killed, perhaps hoping to find their own identity.

A substantial number of survivors have experienced that – after trying to forget through working hard – memories take over in such a way and with such a force that psychological problems become inevitable. All varieties of material and emotional help were made available for this injured group. The results of the persecutions – the so-called 'post-concentration camp or K.Z. syndrome' and other war traumas – were treated in a special clinic, where victims of a prolonged period of hiding also received treatment.[10] Compared with other countries, the degree of psychological assistance is high in Holland. The growing interest in the rescuers, who are honoured by Yad Vashem with ceremonies, awarding of medals, planting of trees, etc., is indicative of the same renewed attention for the victims of the Holocaust.

Jews are now living in a multicultural Dutch society, where they seem well-integrated. In spite of pessimistic prognoses that the Jewish community was doomed to vanish, their number is now estimated at 35,000, compared with 460,000 Muslims and 80,000 Hindus and Buddhists. Their number has not diminished since the war; instead, Jewish traditions are being revived, 50 years later, not only in Amsterdam, but also in the provinces of Holland, where recently synagogues have been restored. Fifty years later, there seems to be a new generation that wants to rid itself of the burden of the past and wants to get on in a new Jewish social context.

Nevertheless, Presser's remark that in a sense all European Jews are survivors of the Holocaust is more than demonstrated by Dutch post-war literature. Not only is the war – with issues like resistance and collaboration – the most 'popular' subject in general literature, the Holocaust is the theme par excellence for Jewish authors, such as those who experienced these events as a child: the before mentioned Marga Minco and Frans Pointl.

Frans Pointl represents in his stories, which in their soberness remind us distantly of Marga Minco's novels, the haunted life of the survivors. Their life is mutilated by the Holocaust and is an accumulation of failures; the schlemiel is the main character in his stories. His is a world full of the kind of anti-heroes we know from the works of Saul Bellow, Bernard Malamud and Philip Roth. Mostly, they are victims of a dominant mother and a hostile, sometimes antisemitic, but always indifferent society. His own mother, who survived with only two of her possessions: *me and her old Steinbach piano*, joined a group of Jewish spiritists to surround herself with the souls of those who had been murdered. In the story *Het tweede licht* (The Second Light), we read about his mother:

> Often she woke me up in the middle of the night with her screaming, or perhaps she was delirious. She called her parents, my grandmother and grandfather, whom I remembered well, and Aunt Henriette, Martha, Salomon, Serah. There were names that did not mean anything either (...) Frightened and with bated breath I used to listen to that dance of death in her dehumanized voice. Then she got up, dreaming as she walked and pulled the large suitcase from under her bed. 'Razzia, razzia!', she screamed. I was afraid that Mrs. Joha, the landlady, would threaten again to put us out into the street, 'if that stupid screaming at night doesn't stop.' I stopped my mother, pulled her roughly by her long grey hair and called: 'Quiet, quiet!', as if she was a bolting mare. I put my mouth to her ear: 'It is nineteen-forty-six and it is over!' (Pointl, 1995:22, own translation)

Just as Pointl's mother, the parents of Ischa Meijer were so marked by their experiences that they brought him up in a cold and distant way. Ischa Meijer was born during the war as a son of the well-known author of many studies on the history of Dutch Jewry, Jaap Meijer. In *Brief aan mijn moeder* (Letter to My Mother) he dealt with his parents and reproached them for the silence that has dominated their lives. The war period had become a taboo that was always referred to in coded language – which they prefered to keep secret.[11] Travelling in the USA, he observed that not everybody deals with his/her camp past in that way:

> "Bergen Belsen", I said to the man at the desk, in the hotel near Times Square. "Belsen!" he said. "Don't make me laugh! Sobibor, that was something. That's where I was." Two people working at a desk behind his back looked up. One said: "Sobibor! You mean Auschwitz!" and he pointed at the number written on his arm.

The other said "Treblinka!" and looked proud.
I felt completely inferior. (Meijer, 1974:22, own translation)

In a public lecture, called *A case of unadapted behaviour*, Meijer described the taboo of talking about the camps:

> After my parents and I returned from concentration camp Bergen-Belsen, my father and mother built – equally unconsciously as carefully – a new camp of their own. Maybe they had not grown more neurotic than they had been before the war, but they had definitely learnt a thing or two. I dare say that my parents had become masters in the art of adapting. (ICODO INFO, 1995:27, own translation)

This ties in neatly with another typical author of the 'second generation': Carl Friedman, born in 1952. She considers herself just as much a victim of the Nazis as the father in her novel *Nightfather*, who cannot stop telling stories about the camp. "I've had camp," as in disease, is the sentence he uses for his K.Z. syndrome and with which he frequently chastises his children. With sober descriptions full of short unadorned sentences, the book reminds us of Minco and Oberski, even though it is more furious. She describes a typical scene between her brother and her parents:

> "It's not true!" shouts Max. "All you love is your SS. When we're at the dinner table, you go on about starvation. When we have a cold, you go on about typhus. Other fathers play soccer in the street with their kids, but when I bring a friend home just once, all you can do is talk about the camp. The camp this, the camp that, always the camp. Why didn't you damn well stay there!" (Friedman, 1994:97)

Her book is a perfect illustration of the war that did not end in May 1945 and even dominates the life of those who were not yet born then.

With another young author, Arnon Grunberg (born in 1971), this is no longer so, although the Shoah clearly dominates the world of his parents. Grunberg is obviously less stricken with the events of 50 years ago. His first novel, *Blauwe Maandagen* (Blue Mondays), is seen as the promising voice of a new generation. For him, the war begins and ends with his parents.

*

In conclusion it is appropriate to cite the man who lived his life in the shadow of yesterday. Jacques Presser, the author who wanted to testify with all means at his disposal – as historian, poet and author – ends his historical study about the destruction of Dutch Jewry with a poem:

Con Sordino

So he returned and had to
speak the language of the living again
in strange gardens undestroyed
tilt his own late roses,
break his bread at foreign tables
after work again like before hard.

He was then not that injured
like some supposed;
it was wrongfully assumed
that his memories plagued him,
or was he indeed one of those heroes
that walk through fires unharmed?
Maybe, maybe; he spoke that language,
he did that work; he seemed to live;
all that is true. Even though only once,
people say, whilst picking roses
a word, a sound made his hands tremble:
but maybe even that is only a story. (Presser, 1965:71, own translation)

The verb 'pulsen' would get a very ominous ring in the ears of many Dutchmen

Anne Frank and her Diary

On the afternoon of that 4 August 1944, after the inhabitants of 'Het Achterhuis' (The Annexe) were taken away, Miep Gies and two other employees of Opekta went up into the hiding-place. They found all the signs of a hasty departure: clothes lying around, chairs fallen over, drawers emptied out, beds turned up; on the floor lots of papers. Miep recognised sheets of Anne's handwriting and picked them up, realising Anne would want them back when she returned. Back in her office, she put them in a drawer of her desk. In doing this, she overstepped the mark, as all Jewish property was automatically confiscated and became 'property of the Reich'. The usual procedure after an arrest was that a removal firm by the name of Puls[12] would come after two or three days and take everything out. In the meantime, the place was locked up. This was indeed what happened, but the diary remained undetected. It was left in its drawer for the rest of the war.

After the capitulation of the German Armies in Holland on 5 May 1945, Miep Gies and her husband Jan waited for the Franks to come back. On 3 June Otto Frank returned to Amsterdam via Odessa and Marseille; he had been liberated on 27 January by the advancing Russian armies. He moved in with Jan and Miep Gies. He knew his wife was dead, but as he said to Miep, 'I have great hope for Anne and Margot.' When he received news of the fate of his two daughters, at the end of July or beginning of August 1945, Miep Gies handed him the papers belonging to his daughter. After he had read them, he made a copy, omitting what could prove offensive to people who were still alive and a few remarks about Anne's mother that 'didn't concern anyone else'. The rest he translated into German and sent to his mother, who was living in Basle, Switzerland. Friends to whom he showed the typescript convinced him he should try and have it published. That was not easy; several big publishers turned it down, until the historian Jan Romein wrote an article on it in one of the daily newspapers under the title, A Child's Voice. The article stated that among the hundreds of diaries in the State Institute for War Documentation, it would be difficult to find one as lucid, as intelligent, and at the same time as natural. It ended:

> *If all the signs do not deceive me, this girl would have become a talented writer had she remained alive. Having arrived here at the age of four from Germany, she was able within ten years to write enviably pure and simple Dutch, and showed an insight into the failings of human nature – her own not excepted – so infallible that it would have astonished one in an adult, let alone in a child. At the same time she also highlighted the infinite possibilities of human nature, reflected in humor, tenderness and love... (The Critical Edition, 1989:67/68)*

The small publishing house of Contact then published the diary in June 1947 in an edition of 1500 copies under the title Het Achterhuis *(The Annexe). Anne's dream had become reality.*

The book met with moderate success: reviews were favourable, but sales were slow in the beginning. The second edition appeared in December 1947, the third in February 1948, the fourth in September 1948, the fifth in February 1949, the sixth in July 1950. The time lapse between February 1949 and July 1950 gave the publisher the impression that interest in the Second World War was declining, and the book was not reprinted between 1950 and 1955. With the commemoration of 10 years of liberation approaching, the seventh edition was published in April 1955 and the eighth in July 1955. After that date, the reprints, translations and new editions followed each other in quick succession.

Also in 1955, a stage adaptation of the diary by Frances Goodrich and Albert Hackett opened with great success on Broadway.[13] The same couple wrote the script for the 1958 film by George Stevens, with Millie Perkins as Anne Frank. All the attention inevitably led to more publications, which in their turn created new interest. In 1958 Ernst Schnabel published the biography Anne Frank. Spur eines Kindes *(translated into English as* The Footsteps of Anne Frank*), in which he interviewed (among others) Otto Frank, Miep and Jan Gies, Hannah Goslar and Janny Brandes-Brilleslijper.*

In 1957 the Anne Frank Foundation was established in Amsterdam and acquired the house, which was opened to the public in May 1960. It would attract an ever growing number of visitors.

Since then, Anne Frank and her diary have become household names all over the world: streets, schools, children's homes, youth hostels, etc. carry her name. She has become an icon of the Holocaust, her face that of millions of anonymous other victims.

When Otto Frank died in Switzerland on 19 August 1980, he left the original diaries to the The Netherlands State Institute for War Documentation. The Institute decided to make a thorough investigation of these papers in response to the growing rumours that there was something wrong with the authorship of the diaries. These rumours originated mainly with the growth of the so-called 'revisionist' movement, a group of people who denied the Holocaust, disputed the existence of the gas chambers, and claimed that the diary of Anne was, in fact, written by Otto Frank; these allegations have increased considerably since the second half of the 1970s.

When the so-called Critical Edition *of more than 700 pages was published in 1986 (English edition 1989), it seemed there was very little left about the life of Anne Frank that was not known. It contained a thorough analysis of her handwriting and of the texture of the paper and ink used to write the diary on. There were articles by staff members of the Institute on the family history of the Franks, their arrest, their betrayal, their deportation; and it presented three slightly different versions of the diary: the first was as Anne had originally written it, the second as she had revised and prepared it for publication herself, and the third as it was published in 1947 with some corrections and omissions by Otto Frank, in cooperation with Contact Publishers.*

For a while, it seemed that with this scholarly edition the last word on Anne Frank and her diaries had been spoken. What could anybody still add that was not yet known? Yet since the publication of the Critical Edition, *at least seven books have been published on her.*

In 1987 Miep Gies, the helper of the Frank family, published her own memoirs with the help of the author Alison Leslie Gold, under the title, Anne Frank Remembered. *The book tells the story of the eight people in hiding, but it gives a lot more than that. Not only do we get a different perspective on the problems of going into hiding, this time from the people on the outside, we also hear about the life of Miep Gies herself as well. Born Hermine Santrouschitz in Vienna, she came to Holland as a small Austrian girl after the collapse of the monarchy and the subsequent chaos, following the defeat in the First World War. She stayed on in Holland, and in 1933 she came to work for Otto Frank as a typist/receptionist. She and her husband-to-be, Jan Gies, became friends of the family. During the war Otto Frank confided in her and asked her to help when the family went into hiding. From July 1942 to August 1944, she looked after the people in the secret annexe, sharing their joys and fears. In 1988 Eva Schloss wrote* Eva's Story, *subtitled* A Survivor's Tale *by the Stepsister of Anne Frank. Anne Frank never really had a stepsister: but after Otto Frank and Elfriede Markovits married in 1953, Eva posthumously became Anne's stepsister. The book tells a story in many ways similar to that of Anne Frank. Born as Eva Geiringer in Vienna in 1929, one month before Anne, her parents and their two children (they also had a son, Heinz, three years her senior) fled Austria in June 1938, first to Breda and then to Amsterdam in 1940. They lived at Merwedeplein 46, while the Franks lived at no. 37. There she saw a trio of girls – Anne, Hanne(li Goschlar) and Sanne (Susanne Lederman) – but they did not want to play with her, because they thought her childish. That is, at least, what Eva thought. In July 1942 her older brother was 'called up' for a labour camp in Germany, just like Margot Frank, and the parents decided it was time to go into hiding. Father and son went to one address, mother and daughter to another.*

On 11 May 1944 – Eva's 15th birthday – they were all arrested after having been betrayed and taken to prison. Two days later, the family was transported to Westerbork and the next day to Auschwitz-Birkenau. In January 1945 she and her mother were freed by the Russian army. Her father and brother had been taken on one of the last SS death marches out of the camp. They had not been heard of since.

Also in 1988 Willy Lindwer published De laatste zeven maanden *(English edition* The Last Seven Months, *1991), the complete interviews of a television documentary of the same name. It is the story of six women (a seventh, Anita Mayer-Roos, published her own story in 1981 and is not included in the book), who all met Anne after she was arrested and went, as she did, to Westerbork, Auschwitz or Bergen-Belsen.*

Another important contribution is that of Janny Brandes-Brilleslijper. She looked after Margot and Anne in the last days of their lives. They both suffered from typhoid, and she watched them grow weaker and weaker by the day.

All these accounts are remarkable stories of hardship and survival beyond comprehension. They all add a little to our knowledge of what happened after that fateful 4 August 1944.

In 1990 Anne en Jopie – Leven met Anne Frank *(Anne and Jopie – Life with Anne Frank) was published by Jaqueline van Maarsen, her friend from secondary school days. The book seems to have been written only to contradict* Eva's Story. *Jaqueline van Maarsen, Jaque in the original diary and Jopie de Waal in the 1947 edition, was a good friend of Anne's. She is referred to many times in the diary, for instance on 15 June 1942:*

> *In the meantime I have met Jopie de Waal at the Jewish Lyceum. We are together a lot and she is my best friend now.*

How quickly 13-year-old girls can change their minds is apparent from the entry four days later:

> *Jaque is all of a sudden very taken with Ilse and behaves very childishly and stupidly towards me. I like her less and less.*

Nevertheless, she is referred to many times after as a best friend, so it is clear she was an important figure in Anne's circle. She was the daughter of a Jewish father and a non-Jewish, French mother. Her mother converted to Judaism, but managed to undo that later in the war, thus saving not only her two daughters, but her husband, too.

In the same year – 1990 – the historian Nanda van der Zee published De kamergenoot van Anne Frank *(Anne Frank's Roommate), about the dentist Fritz Pfeffer. The book is based upon the find – by Joke Kniesmeijer of the Anne Frank Foundation – of a couple of photo albums at the Waterlooplein flea-market in 1987. In a couple of the photos, she recognised the dentist Dr Albert Dussel as he is called in Anne's diary, with whom she shared a room in the 'Achterhuis'. His real name was Fritz Pfeffer. Nanda van der Zee wanted to write a book about this dental surgeon from Berlin, whom she thought had come off rather badly in the diary, and decided to use this find.*

Fritz Pfeffer had been divorced from his first wife when he met the non-Jewish Charlotte Kaletta, also divorced and 19 years his junior. In 1938 they fled from Germany and moved to Amsterdam. In November 1942 he went into hiding with the Franks and the Van Pels; Charlotte, being non-Jewish, did not need to go into hiding and never saw him again. On 20 December 1944 he died in Neuengamme concentration camp.

Apart from a photo-biography, Anne Frank, *by staff members of the Anne Frank Foundation, Ruud van der Rol and Rian Verhoeven, published in 1992, and a new 1995 edition of the* Diary of Anne Frank, *based upon the* Critical Edition, *there is the Dutch translation of an original German publication* Anne Frank was niet alleen *(Anne Frank Was Not Alone), published in 1990. It is of interest because it contains interviews with German Jews, who, like Anne Frank, came to Holland in the Thirties. Finally, there is also a Dutch translation of another originally German book,* Daar verlang ik zo naar *(That's What I Long for so much), published in 1993, by Mirjam Pressler. The latter is a personal interpretation of the diary and of the personalities of the eight people in the 'Achterhuis'.*

We feel it is no exaggeration to say that Anne Frank has become the symbol of senseless suffering in the Second World War, the Holocaust, the six million Jews who died in the concentration camps. The sheer size of that number defies all imagination; nobody is capable of visualizing six million dead. Anne Frank gives them a face. Her diary has been translated into more than 50 languages, and more than 20 million copies have been sold. There are plays, films, TV documentaries. The 'Achterhuis' was made into a museum, which is visited by more than 600,000 people annually.

We need to ask the questions: Why this girl? Why this diary? Why Anne Frank? There are many different answers to these questions, but let us consider S. Dresden's opinion in his latest book, Vervolging, Vernietiging, Literatuur *(Persecution, Destruction, Literature), in which he argues that her descriptions of suffering are not extreme enough to justify making her into a symbol of Jewish suffering. He quotes Arnoni, himself a survivor, with obvious approval:*

> What I had read I found particularly moving. What I revolted at is that this book was seen as typical of the Jewish persecution and in that way became popular. Typical it is not at at all... The overwhelming majority, the millions in ghettos, labour camps, extermination camps, underwent a fate that was essentially so much sadder... that they cannot be symbolized by what she had to say. (Dresden, 1995:197,198)

Dresden adds as an afterthought that there is very little talk in the diary of typically Jewish elements. That might make it more acceptable in a universal human sense, but at the same time it does not make it a particularly fitting symbol for the Jewish suffering.

Of course, Anne Frank cannot be blamed for her popularity. Besides she was herself aware of her relatively privileged and safe position in the hiding-place. On 2 May 1943 she wrote:

> When I sometimes think about how we live here, I usually conclude that in comparison to other Jews who haven't gone into hiding, we live as if in paradise...

VII
The Epilogue

It has happened,
and so it can happen again;
it can happen,
everywhere
(Primo Levi)

I did not study the question, but I believe it (i.e. the Holocaust) is but a small *detail* (statement by Jean-Marie Le Pen, leader of the French right wing party Le Front National, on 13 September 1987)

The difference between 'history' and 'literature' is sometimes interpreted as the difference between 'fact' and 'fiction', or even between 'truth' and 'fantasy'. We would like to argue here that in order to begin to understand the events we call the Holocaust, the literature of those events must be seen as an important historical source. If we want to penetrate that mystery of collective behaviour, ordinary knowledge of history does not suffice. Bare facts, horrific though they are, are meaningless unless they are given significance by personal testimony. The personal experiences of Gerard Durlacher, Jona Oberski and all the other writers we have met were set in the context of 'the history'. The experience of the Holocaust transcends the limitations of both traditional disciplines of history and literature.

The Polish/American author Louis Begley, author of the pseudo-auto-biographical novel *Wartime Lies*, stated in an interview[1] that he found it difficult to talk about himself. Therefore, he invented a 'hero' and made him live through the same kind of experiences he had lived through himself:

> I needed the intervention of a literary form to make use of personal recollections. The literary form enables one to add things, to idealize them or to change them. I was looking for an artistic truth that would not violate historical truth. (own translation)

Begley needed an invented *artistic* truth to supplement what he considered to be an incomplete *historical* truth. To a certain extent this might be true for all literature, but we feel that it is within the field of Holocaust literature that these questions are particularly relevant.

The literature of the Holocaust is often referred to as a 'literature of silence' or a 'literature of the unspeakable', meaning that silence can be the only appropriate answer to the events in the death camps of Nazi Germany.

George Steiner's often quoted dictum '*The world of Auschwitz lies outside speech as it lies outside reason*' illustrates this point of view.[2] The incomprehensible dimensions of the *war against the Jews* doom every effort to present it in words.

The problem of expression when dealing with the Holocaust is not the consequence of inadequate philosophical profoundness, but of lack of power. Words will always fail when very deep emotions are at stake. The Holocaust is everything but a metaphysical event; it can be understood, the Hungarian author Imre Kertész maintains. He compares his own obsessive talking about Auschwitz to a 'silence in words'. Maybe Auschwitz is of a completely different order than all other cruelties in history, as Hannah Arendt and others have suggested. But that does not make Nazism in itself unununderstandable, not even the gassings, as De Jong and other historians emphasize. The Holocaust, caused by human beings, is as understandable as any other historical event. We can to a certain degree 'understand' the victims, the bystanders, and, be it with more difficulty, the perpetrators.[3]

Nevertheless, only a very few historians have dared to explore fully the why of the Holocaust. Maybe we have to accept this failure as the logical consequence of an 'unmasterable past', just as, paradoxically, the obsessive need to remember is.

Israeli historian Saul Friedlander concluded that there may be no other solution to this unsolvable problem:

> The inability to say, the apparent pathology of obsessive recall, the seemingly simplistic refusal of historiographical closure may ultimately be the only self-evident sequels of an unmasterable past. (Friedlander, 1993:62)

Every effort to speak would be an effort to explain the inexplicable. That is the point Elie Wiesel made when he stated in *Confronting the Holocaust* (the chapter is called *Why I write*):

> There is no such thing as a literature of the Holocaust, nor can there be. The very expression is a contradiction in terms...A novel about Auschwitz is not a novel or else it is not about Auschwitz. The very attempt to write such a novel is blasphemy.

According to Wiesel, any attempt to fictionalise Auschwitz borders by necessity on blasphemy. The reality of the death camps cannot bear the embellishment Wiesel thinks is inevitable in fiction. Others, notably Claude Lanzmann and Shoshana Felman, even go so far as to maintain that the only possible ethical attitude towards the Holocaust is '*the refusal of understanding*'. Every attempt to explain it is an attempt to reduce it.

There are numerous survivors who have stated that only numbed and wounded silence can do justice to the millions of dead and even more significantly to the handful of survivors, the witnesses of a crime about which they were not supposed to testify. But, as Primo Levi rightly remarked about the survivors: there are those who remain silent, and there are those who tell a story. *Forgetting is the Final Solution* appears as the last line of a discussion about this subject in Theo Richmond's book, *Konin: A Quest*. Greet van Amstel expressed a similar opinion in a poem:

> Every murdered person is a prosecutor,
> there are millions of prosecutors.
> They cannot remain silent.
> To remain silent
> is to become accessory.
> (Van Amstel, 1965:6, own translation)

Or, as stated by the historian Jacques Presser who describes his decision to write his magnum opus about the Holocaust in Holland: *His choice was only to write or to remain silent. He chose to write, his heart demanded it. For the rest, the reader must be his judge.*

In this book we gave voice to people such as Presser, for whom writing was the answer to the massive trauma undergone by the Holocaust victims. They answered the question of whether it is possible to write about the Holocaust at all with an emphatic 'yes', and their testimonies lie at the centre of our book. Their contributions may in fact throw another light on the discussion about the possibility of adequately representing the Holocaust in written form – a topic which lies outside the scope of this book, having been treated quite extensively elsewhere.[4]

Again, it needs to be stressed that we made but a small selection of the 'ego-documents' written by Dutch Jewry. In Holland, too, there is a mountain of literature about the Holocaust, fiction as well as non-fiction, making the years between 1933 and 1945 the best documented period in the country's history. It is indeed *eine Vergangenheit die nicht vergehen will* (a past that will not go away), to quote the title of Ernst Nolte's famous article in the *Frankfurter Allgemeine Zeitung* that launched the *Historikerstreit* (Historians' Debate) of the Eighties on the unprecedented nature of the Holocaust.

When even the perpetrators, the camp commandant of Westerbork, Gemmeker, for instance, felt the need to record the events they witnessed, how can one expect the victims not to testify? Theodor Adorno's by now almost trivial statement – that the writing of poetry after Auschwitz would be barbaric – was not only later amended by himself but also – in a way – refuted by the survivors themselves who wrote about their experiences. Obviously indescribable is not the same as saying something cannot be written about.

Yet, all we have to get 'inside' the Holocaust are images and words, fiction and non-fiction. One is reminded of Maurice Blanchot's *L'écriture du désastre* (The Writing of the Disaster), where he writes: *Since the disaster always takes place after having taken place, there cannot possibly be any experience of it.* (Blanchot, 1986:28)

Only when we begin to look for the right words to describe what happened does the experience turn into reality. However, as we have no previous experience of it, it is a testing and probing search. We cannot believe our own ears, we cannot trust our own words, our memory is unreliable. That is why the distinction Charlotte Delbo made between 'vrai' and 'véridique' is so much to the point. How do we know something is true (= vrai), when we have no words for the events we have to recount, when those words themselves belie the experiences?

Durlacher tried to express the same feeling:

> When we arrived home, we turned out to be travelers with an impoverished vocabulary. We lacked the language to describe our experiences. The worn-out words that did exist did not get uttered, for virtually nobody was there to hear them and virtually nobody wanted to listen to them, let alone try to comprehend them. (Durlacher,1991:99)

Durlacher wrote these words as a response to the period after the war, during which Dutch people wanted to forget, when what had happened to the Jews fell on deaf ears. But now that those times have changed and virtually everybody wants to know, the inability to represent the unrepresentable only seems to have become more poignant. In the last two decades more than twice as many survivor memoirs have been published than appeared in the first 20 years after the war, and that is not just true of Holland.

Let us cite one example. In 1994 the French writer Sarah Kofman described in a little book of 70 pages, *Rue Ordener, rue Labat*, the deportation of her father (a rabbi in Paris), her own going into hiding with her mother at a Christian woman's apartment, the subsequent estrangement from her mother and the postwar consequences – in short, all the problems we have explored in our book. The first page of the book is devoted to the fountain-pen, the only object that is left of her deported father: *Je le possède toujours, rafistolé avec du scotch, il est devant mes yeux sur ma table de travail et il me contraint à écrire, écrire* (I still have it, wrapped with scotch-tape, lying before my eyes on my desk and it forces me to write, to write). And write she did, thousands of pages on art, literature, psychoanalysis, philosophy (Nietzsche) and antisemitism. She had to write these thousands of pages to be able at last to write the 70 pages, *pour parvenir à raconter 'ça'* (to end up telling 'that'). But these 70 pages impart meaning to all her previous books. Having published her little book, she committed suicide. Perhaps this was inevitable, not unlike the suicides of survivors like Tadeusz Borowski, Jean Améry and Primo Levi after they unburdened themselves of their testimonies.

Many of the survivors we have met felt a similar urge to tell 'that', frequently after many years of exemplary work in other fields. All of them, with the exception of the much older Herzberg, remained silent for a long time about 'that' and only published their memoirs, either as diaries or as fiction, much later. Even if they did not have a fountain-pen left from their beloved ones, sooner or later there apparently appeared that urge to write which overcame any moral, philosophical or literary doubts.

It is irrelevant that some of the testimonies are more 'literary' than others. In general, we used memoirs of people who had little difficulty expressing themselves on paper. None set out to write 'literature' as such, even if the need for a literary style is evident in all of them. Some would certainly agree with Yugoslav author Danilo Kiš, who considered style imperative in the interpretation of the most gruesome events. Durlacher described his motivation to write down his memories, after repressing them for three decades: *You have to find a literary form to engrave it in their memory, otherwise it will later only be of interest to historians.*[5]

Apparently, he and others did not want to reach historians only. Most had a moral and didactic aim in mind. Some of the chroniclers of life in the ghettos of Eastern Europe repeatedly emphasized that their aim was to record for posterity, so that their lives had not been in vain, which explains why they took the pains they did to make sure their writings would survive them.

Others wanted to ensure that the guilt of the perpetrators was laid down in words for all eternity. This was the case with Mirjam Blits, who wrote: *I would like to fill you with hatred against everything SS and Nazi. Hatred against them who despised me so terribly and have made me so unhappy.* (We would like to mention that she wrote these words shortly after her return from Auschwitz.)

Many camp survivors, among them Primo Levi and Elie Wiesel, were afraid that they would not be believed. The more extreme their experiences, the greater this fear. Herzberg, for instance, is very much aware of the exceptional nature of his experiences. When writing *Tweestroomenland* (Land of Two Streams)[6], his diary in Bergen-Belsen, it is as if he knows that one day he would write the chronicle of the persecution of the Jews in Holland[7], just as De Jong felt the vocation to write the history of his country under Nazi occupation while still in London (little did he know that his work would become a comprehensive study of Dutch society in all its facets).

Most of them were motivated by more subjective feelings as well. Anne Frank wrote on June 20, 1942, that she began to write in her diary after having given the matter significant thought. The reason she gave was that she did not have a friend in whom she could confide completely:

> ...I don't want to set down a series of bald facts in a diary like most people do, but I want this diary itself to be my friend, and I shall call my friend Kitty (Frank, 1989: 180)

For the people in the camps, keeping a diary was a way of imposing order on an unknown and alien world, where reasons and arguments counted for very little. Intellectuals for the most part, they used words to regain control over disorder, to master the chaos to whatever extent possible. Intellectually and psychologically, theirs was a method of self-preservation and self-assertion.[8] *The daily struggle against the disgust of communal life, against noise and triviality and vulgarity uses up a lot of energy. In writing I found a diversion which often helped me to forget the disgust*, wrote Mechanicus on 30 October 1943. These reasons were more important than the conditions under which they lived, which were everything but conducive – because of personal danger or lack of the necessary tools – to write with some frequency. Renata Laqueur:

> Why do I keep this diary? If it is found here, I will be punished severely; and when the war is over nobody will want to hear about this misery anymore. Maybe they will even say it is all exaggerated. Yet I continue in order to avoid complete numbness and to try and stay on top of the daily routine. (Laqueur, 1965:21)

However difficult their lives, they were out of sorts when they neglected their diary, like David Koker: *It is annoying when I lose my sense of style, my eye for detail and proportion. I want to try and work more regularly at it again in the evenings.* (Koker, 1977:75)

*

Jacques Presser made a useful distinction when he described the difference between the 'external' diary in which the author records observations, facts and events, and the 'intimate' one, filled with reflections and individual responses.[9]

David Koker had what he himself called an *analytical interest in concentration camp phenomenons* (Koker, 1977:151). Although elements of the 'external' diary are not completely absent, he did not mean to write his diary for that purpose. Neither he nor Loden Vogel are primarily out to record the events in the camp. They are interested in their own personal experiences and their responses to them. Why? In the first place for themselves; for later, after their return, or simply, as Moshe Flinker wrote: *It is because I hate being idle that I have started this diary so that I can write in it every day what I do and think* (Flinker, 1965:23).

Vogel hardly even seems to concern himself with life in the camp. Out of self-preservation he restricted himself in his intimate diary to observations about his own frame of mind and the reactions of a small circle of family and friends. He *used psychoanalytic language and recorded his associations as they might come to him on a psychiatrist's couch.*[10] Where others thought only of food, he was writing a camp diary to maintain his mental stability.[11] A sense of humor and self-mockery came in handy: *My sense of humor, the way I look at things, is much more real than before: a mask then, now part of the harness.*

As documents about life in Bergen-Belsen the 'external' diaries of Herzberg and Laqueur have no equal; as the diary of Mechanicus will remain the most complete source of information about Westerbork. *I feel like as if I am an official reporter giving an account of a shipwreck*, wrote Philip Mechanicus on May 29, 1943. Like the other diarists he also felt he had *a duty to continue writing*, even if for no other reason than to inform *those who want to have an idea of what has happened here.*

As a 'document humain' the diary of Loden Vogel has a special place in the literature of the Holocaust, like the diaries of David Koker, Moshe Flinker, Anne Frank and Etty Hillesum. David Koker stands out for his down-to-earth intelligence:

> It is nonsense to expect any form of happiness in this period. All that matters is to preserve one's possibilities. One can deepfreeze all one's emotions, afterwards one can defrost them and then they are alive again...
>
> Of late, I often think about that line (of Rilke's): 'Wer spricht von Siegen? Ueberstehn ist alles.' (Who talks about winning? All that matters is getting through). Everything, certainly our relations with our friends, is an effort to try to maintain earlier relationships, aimed at resuming those relationships in their original form after the war. Our whole life here is formal. Our relationship to others: a form without content. Not to worry: as long as the form is there, everything is alright. In the future everything will be filled in again.

Koker goes on to say that it would be too exhausting to live this kind of life consciously:

> Hibernation would be better (...) It might have been a time of experiences. But so little penetrates our consciousness. Possibly everything is being bottled up in our consciousness, and it will come out after the war. To activate those unconscious experiences, that must be the task of this diary...(Koker, 1977:126-127, own translation)

The last pages of these diaries often are the most moving, knowing that the authors of these lines would not survive. Etty Hillesum, in her last letter, also wrote about 'after the war', but clearly with a more idealistic vision:

> I have told you often enough that no words and images are adequate to describe nights like these. But still I must try to convey something of it to you. One always has the feeling here of being the ears and eyes of a piece of Jewish history, but there is also the need sometimes to be a still, small voice. We must keep one another in touch with everything that happens in the various outposts of this world, each one contributing his own little piece of stone to the great mosaic that will take shape once the war is over. (Hillesum, 1983:207-208)

These last words hint at a moral obligation, a debt we owe to those who did not return. Perhaps we should leave the last words to Herzberg:

Homo homini homo. This is not only the motto of this small book (i.e. *The night of the Girondists* by Jacques Presser), it also stands in invisible letters above Westerbork, and Auschwitz, and Bergen-Belsen...Homo homini homo. It stands everywhere where people are really put to the test. Above our heads and in our hearts, and maybe, maybe, we can hope that if it penetrates deep enough, it can protect us from further trials. (Herzberg, 1996:232, own translation)

Notes

Notes to Chapter I

1   To be precise, before 1579 there were 17 very small Low Countries, with Holland and Flanders as the two most important ones. In that year seven Northern Provinces decided to go their own way in their fight for independence against Spain, while a number of Southern provinces made their peace with the Spanish king. From 1648 onwards this situation was confirmed in the Peace Treaty of Westfalia. The North continued under the name *Republic of the Seven United Provinces*, most commonly called Holland after its most powerful component, the South continued under foreign rulers – Spain, Austria, France – until, after Napoleon, the two parties of before 1579 were united again. This reunion only lasted 15 years: in 1830 the South stood up against the North and seceded under the name Kingdom of Belgium. To avoid further confusion we will in general use the name 'Holland', being the most familiar, instead of The Netherlands.

2   It has often been assumed that there is a direct link between antisemitism and Jewish prowess in trade. Since trade enjoyed considerable respectability in Holland, unlike in Germany and Eastern Europe, the absence of this motivation for virulent antisemitism might go some way to explain the relative freedom of Jews in Holland. Another explanation for the Dutch tradition of tolerance might be found in its strong decentralist tradition with its preparedness to accept different religious and political convictions. In this respect the Dutch Republic had much in common with the USA, like Holland sprung from a revolt against suppression. The Dutch model of a pluralist nation influenced the Founding Fathers of the USA. There are interesting similarities between the theoretical foundations of the American Constitution and the Dutch 'Acte van Verlatinghe' (1581), the theoretical justification to rise against the King of Spain. However, the Americans learnt from the weaknesses of the Dutch federal system and opted for a strong executive power.

3   Since the end of the Middle Ages, almost all professions had themselves organized in 'guilds', professional organisations that regulated training, production methods and competition. Only guild members could practise a trade; moonlighting was strictly prohibited. Since membership was reserved to those who had passed the master test, it was easy to exclude certain categories from membership. The guilds ceased to exist in 1795.

4   However, the Dutch historian Johan Huizinga did express the same kind of pessimism in his book *In de schaduwen van morgen* (In the Shadows of Tomorrow) in 1935.

5   Menno ter Braak was one of the founders of the Committee of Vigilance that wanted to warn against the danger of Fascism and Nazism. He had therefore no illusions about what would happen in Holland after a German invasion. He committed suicide in May 1940.

Notes to Chapter II

1   That was in 1938, and in 1940 Wielek did indeed think of them. The book, published in 1947, represents the first monument to the Jewish victims in Holland and is a direct predecessor of the works of Herzberg, Presser and De Jong. The idea of providing a record of the anti-Jewish policies of the German authorities originated with two journalists during the war. Both were deported and did not return. H. Wielek (real name Willy Kwikselber, 1912-1988) was asked to finish what they had started. Born in Cologne, he fled to Holland in 1933 and therefore knew the problems of the refugees and the Jews of Holland from his own experience.

2   On the Joodsche Raad see Dan Michman "The Uniqueness of the Joodse Raad in the Western European Context" in J. Michman (ed.), *Dutch Jewish History* t.III (Jerusalem 1993), 371-380.

3   *The Jewish problem does not exist...but what does exist is an antisemitic problem*, wrote the illegal student paper cited above.

4   As a result of the 'dejudification' of the provinces, from April 1943 on, only Amsterdam would be open for Jews.

5   This is the literal translation of the Dutch text. In the 1995 Macmillan edition of the diary this reads: *You're scared to do anything, because it may be forbidden.* We preferred the original with the emphasis on the subject, so we decided not to follow the Macmillan translation.

6   After the war, the Jewish Council would be severely criticized for supporting anti-Jewish measures such as the issue of Yellow Stars and for *publishing the Jewish Weekly once it became clear that this publication could only serve German rather than Jewish interests.*

Notes to Chapter III

1   With respect to Nazi policies of deception, see Jacob Boas in *Jaarboek RIOD 5*, 69-96.

2   Even in the USA some people took these threats from Hitler seriously. In a mid-1939 Congressional Testimony the American journalist Quentin Reynolds predicted the 'annihilation' of the Jews in 'a complete pogrom.'

3   Seyss-Inquart is said to have called Rauter *a great child, with all a child's cruelty.* Presser adds sarcastically: *needless to say, the Jews experienced more of his cruelty than of his childishness.* (Presser, 1969:341)

4   In the spring of 1943, the Jews in mixed marriages detained at Westerbork had to choose between two horrible alternatives: deportation or sterilization. Most chose the latter. In a number of cases, the doctors who had to perform the operation managed to evade the order and only made an insignificant cut. The Dutch Churches strongly protested against the sterilization to Seyss-Inquart: *Sterilization constitutes a violation of the divine commandments as well as of human rights. It is the ultimate consequence of an anti-Christian and life-destroying racial doctrine, of overweening arrogance, of an outlook on life that is incompatible with true Christian and human existence...*

5   The German word is *platzen.*

6   Concentration camp Amersfoort was, like Vught, a transition camp for so-called 'punishment cases'. They were awaiting further transport to camps in the Reich like Neuengamme, Buchenwald and Mauthausen, or to forced labour camps. The treatment of the prisoners was harsh, as experienced by the journalist Philip Mechanicus who was severely tortured. In Amersfoort Cohen came into contact with Mechanicus, whom he was to meet later again in Westerbork.

7   See for a comparative analysis: Pim Griffioen and Ron Zeller "Jodenvervolging in Nederland en België tijdens de Tweede Wereldoorlog: een vergelijkende analyse" in *Jaarboek RIOD 8*. Also: J.C.H. Blom "The Persecution of the Jews in the Netherlands: A Comparative Western European Perspective" in *European History Quarterly*, Vol.19(1989), 333-351.

8   The *Hollandsche Schouwburg* was opened in 1892, first as an operetta venue, soon as a theatre for all sorts of productions. In September 1941, it was rebaptized *Joodsche Schouwburg* (Jewish Theatre): admission was limited to Jewish artists and Jewish audiences. In July 1942, the Nazis turned it into an assembly point for the Jews of Amsterdam, before being taken to Westerbork. After the war it was briefly in use as a theater again, under the name of 'Piccadilly'(!), but many thought a building with so many sad memories could no longer be a place of entertainment. In the Fifties nobody really knew what to do with the building; in 1962 it opened as a memorial. In 1993 it was

reopened after a restoration during which the family names of 104,000 murdered Dutch Jews were recorded on a wall.

9   In sharp contrast to the difficulties the resistance organisations experienced in finding hiding places for Jews, we would like to point out that 300,000 young Dutch men eventually found a hiding place to prevent the *Arbeitseinsatz* (forced employment) in Germany. This does not necessarily imply an unwillingness to take in Jews; it also demonstrates an increased efficiency among resistance organisations and a heightened awareness of the dangers that being sent to Germany could involve among the general population.

10   In the edition of the diary Anne began to prepare for publication she calls them Van Daan's; likewise she would call Fritz Pfeffer Dr. Dussel. She did this so as not to embarrass them, in case of a real publication.

11   There is an apocryphal, but characteristic story about an encounter between the arresting officer and Otto Frank. Otto Frank, a 2nd lieutenant in the Imperial German Army of the First World War, kept some of his belongings in his old army box. Seeing this box the officer asked whom it belonged to. After Otto Frank had said it was his, the tone of the officer changed and became more respectful. Even after 25 years and under totally different circumstances, the discipline of the old army still held.

12   Miep Gies tells in her book, *Anne Frank Remembered*, how she tried to bribe this officer, after she had discovered that he came from Vienna, the city from which Miep Gies also originates. She went to see him in his Euterpestraat office, but although he did not seem unwilling to enter into a bargain with her, when she returned he told her there was nothing he could do, since the prisoners had already been taken to the Weteringschans prison.

Notes to Chapter IV

1   *In my awareness, events no longer have a perspective, but stand lined up beside each other, outside of space and time* (Mechanicus, 1968:171). Similar observations can be found in many other camp diaries.

2   In June 1944 the last Jews from Vught were deported directly to Auschwitz. They belonged to this group of so-called Philips Jews.

3   It would not be the very last train from Westerbork: there would still be one train to Theresienstadt and one to Bergen-Belsen.

Notes to Chapter V

1   Only a small number, mostly non-Dutch Jews, were taken from Holland to Buchenwald, Dachau, Neuengamme and the women's camp Ravensbrück. Some so-called *Nacht und Nebel* (Night and Fog) prisoners ended up in concentration camp Struthof-Natzweiler in Alsace-Lorraine, never to be heard of again.

2   The Dutch novelist W.F. Hermans quotes a German as saying: *The greatest blow the Jews dealt Germany was to fill so many of our goods-wagons and cattle-trucks.* In *De donkere kamer van Damocles* (The Dark Room of Damocles), 238.

3   *Kapo* (Capo) is an abbreviation of *Kamppolizei* (camp police), consisting mainly of fellow prisoners. To keep their 'cushy' job, in many camps they rivalled the SS in cruelty and heavy-handed tactics. To survive in the camps, one needed to be on friendly terms with the capos, to have connections. One needed a lot of 'vitamin c' (connections in camp jargon). See on the linguistics of the Third Reich the book of Victor Klemperer: *LTI. Notizbuch eines Philologen* (Leipzig 1966).

4   Source: archives RIOD Amsterdam, file Bergen-Belsen, nr.9/10.

5   The essayist Menachem Arnoni was even more empathetic when he wrote that the most important lesson he had learnt in Auschwitz was that there was an Eichmann hiding in him.

6   Horror scenes of bodies being bulldozed into large pits are included in virtually every documentary on Bergen-Belsen. It is not widely known that the director of the British camera crew filming these scenes was Alfred Hitchcock.

7   During the visit of the Red Cross, its members were also shown a 'school'; it was closed because of the 'summer holidays'. In reality, all school education was strictly forbidden from the beginning.

8   The film has become generally known under this title. The real title was *Theresienstadt, ein Dokumentarfilm aus dem jüdischen Siedlungsgebiet* (Theresien-stadt, a documentary from the Jewish settlement area). Source: K. Margry: "Theresienstadt (1944-1945): the Nazi propaganda film depicting the concentration camp as paradise" in *Historical Journal of Film, Radio and Television*, Vol. 12, nr 2 (1992):145-162.

9   See the study by the Dutch historian of architecture Robert-Jan van Pelt and Debórah Dwork, *Auschwitz. 1270 to the present* (London 1996).

10   Although there are no accurate figures, it is estimated that the Nazis murdered 500,000 gypsies.

11   *Ladies, quickly, quickly, the water turns cold*, belonged to the standard summons
     of one of the Treblinka trial defendants when chasing Jewish women to the
     gas chambers.

12   Hedwig Hoess once remarked to a Polish gardener that in her opinion *the
     Jews must disappear from the face of the earth to the last man, and that at the proper
     time the end of even the English Jews would come* (*KL Auschwitz seen by the SS*,
     Auschwitz, 1994:224).

13   In an interview in *NRC-Handelsblad*, 30 April, 1991. A similar attitude can be
     found in Herzberg's diary from Bergen-Belsen: *Tweestroomenland* (pp.18, 145,
     201, 228). For an analysis of morality in the camps, see among others Tzvetan
     Todorov: *Facing the extreme. Moral life in the concentration camps* (New York,
     1995).

14   Rooms full of suitcases, shoes, spectacles, artificial limbs, toothbrushes, toys,
     hair, etc. in Auschwitz, and these days also in the Holocaust Museum in
     Washington, are the silent witnesses of the many who have not returned.

15   For a more detailed analysis of his motivations, see Yehuda Bauer, *Jews for
     Sale? Nazi-Jewish Negotiations, 1933-1945* (New Haven 1994).

16   As revenge for the killing of Heydrich, the Germans destroyed the Czech
     village of Lidice and murdered all its male inhabitants. More than 2000 Czech
     citizens were to pay with their lives for the murder of Heydrich.

17   In the summer of 1941 Hitler officially stopped the 'Euthanasia' program
     because of the adverse reaction of the German public. Henry Friedlander
     shows that *more victims of euthanasia perished after the stop was issued than before*
     through 'wild' euthanasia. Henry Friedlander, *The origins of Nazi genocide from
     euthanasia to the Final Solution* (Chapel Hill 1995).

18   *Warnings of Genocide*, lecture given at King's College, London, March 31, 1995,
     by Jan Karski.

19   The warning was not heeded. In the summer of 1944, 437,000 Hungarian Jews
     were deported mainly to Auschwitz. Destroying them seemed priority num-
     ber one: with clockwork-like precision the railways worked overtime to get
     the Jews out of Hungary. In spite of efforts by, for instance, Raoul Wallenberg,
     who saved at least 30,000, Hungarian Jewry was obliterated. As a cruel twist
     of fate, the gas chambers of Auschwitz were working at top capacity in
     August 1944, when 24,000 Hungarian Jews were gassed in one day!

20   Churchill himself was one of the first statesmen to grasp the dangers to the
     Jews of a Nazi victory. He had always condemned what Daniel Goldhagen
     called the 'eliminationist' antisemitism of the Nazis in the strongest terms.
     See: Martin Gilbert "The Most Horrible Crime" in *The Times Literary Supple-
     ment*, June 7 1996.
     See for the discussion on the attitude of the Allies: Walter Laqueur: *The Terrible
     Secret*, London, 1982; Martin Gilbert: *Auschwitz and the Allies*, London, 1981;

Walter Laqueur and Richard Breitman: *Breaking the Silence*, London, 1986; David Wyman: *The Abandonment of the Jews. America and the Holocaust 1941-1945*, New York, 1984.

21   Yehuda Bauer, *op. cit.*, 257.

22   With characteristic German precision transport lists of all deportations from Westerbork were kept. They were made up by members of the Jewish Council of Westerbork. These lists – in neat alphabetical order – are an important source of information for the destinations people were sent to. In too many cases, however, that is where all further information stops.

Notes to Chapter VI

1   More often than not, survivors only returned after a long odyssey. Eva Schloss and her mother – who would remarry in 1953 with Otto Frank, Anne's father – returned via Odessa and Istanbul, just like Greet van Amstel, Primo Levi and other survivors of Auschwitz-Birkenau.

2   The last winter of the war, 1944/1945, was one of the coldest of this century. In Holland in September 1944, the Dutch railways went on strike, in response to an appeal made by the government in London. The Germans retaliated with a decree that prohibited the supply of food and fuel to the west of the country. Shortages and starvation were the result. About 15,000 people died of the combined effect of hunger and cold.

3   'Bewariër' is an almost untranslatable play on words. In it we find the Dutch words for Aryan ('ariër') and for keeping, safeguarding ('bewaren'). *Bewary-ans* would come close with its hidden meaning to beware of the Aryan, but it is not the same.

4   Ironically, this was also the name of the Jewish Guardianship Institution that sought to look after the interests of the Jewish war orphans: *Le-Ezrath Ha-Jeled*, In the Interest of the Child. In the battle over these children, it sometimes seemed as if these interests came very low on the list.

5   In Bergen-Belsen his mother had warned him not to kiss anyone in the camp on the lips, because it might be dangerous. Infections could be transferred by a 'kiss of death'.

6   Seyss-Inquart was hanged in Nuremberg, but none of his staff members were ever convicted for their role in the persecution of the Jews.

7   Presser's young wife, Dé, died in Auschwitz. He survived the war by going into hiding.

8   Willy Lages was in charge of the SD in Amsterdam; as such, he was respon-
        sible for the deportations of approximately 70,000 Jews from Amsterdam.

9   The result of this search operation was published in a book and TV documen-
        tary *De Zoektocht* (The Search).

10   It was Elie Cohen, himself a survivor of Auschwitz, who introduced in the
        1960s the so-called 'post-concentratiekampsyndroom' in Holland.

11   See: Ischa Meijer 'Een geval van onaangepast gedrag' (A Case of Unadapted
        Behaviour) in *ICODO INFO 95-3/4*, special issue on 'Children of the War –
        Then and Now – ' p.24-35. In this article Meijer describes his feeling of 'not
        belonging', notwithstanding all the efforts of adaptation and covering up on
        the part of his parents.

12   'Puls' became such a notorious name in wartime Holland that a verb was
        created, to 'puls,' meaning to clean a house out from top to bottom. After the
        war the firm was not allowed to continue in business.

13   The effort to ensure the adaptation rights caused an undignified conflict
        between the author Meyer Levin on the one hand and the screenwriters
        Goodrich and Hackett on the other. It is true that Meyer Levin was responsible
        almost singlehandedly for the publication of the diary in America in 1952. It
        appears that he considered it his right, consequently, to adapt the book into
        a play. However, Otto Frank rejected his version – it is said he found it too
        'Jewish' – and opted for the other one. It would lead to a lifelong feud, court
        cases and bitter articles until the death of Otto Frank in 1980 and of Levin in
        1981.

Notes to Chapter VII

1   *NRC-Handelsblad*, 12th of November 1993.

2   That sentence appears in *K*, an essay on Franz Kafka in *Language and Silence*.
        There Steiner does not elaborate on the point any further, but in another essay
        in the same volume, *The Hollow Miracle*, he writes:
        *Use a language to conceive, organize, and justify Belsen; use it to make specifications
        for gas ovens; use it to dehumanize man during twelve years of calculated bestiality.
        Something will happen to it.* (Steiner, 1969:124)
            The point he wants to make is that a language that has been used to facilitate
        all this cannot at the same time be used to express what has been happening
        at Auschwitz.

3   It is significant that, even fifty years later, so few writers have seriously tried
        to desribe the mind of the perpetrators from inside, whereas the point of view

of the victims is represented abundantly in the literature. One of the few exceptions is the story *The kapo* by the Yugoslavian author Alexander Tišma.

4   See the coverage of this topic in, for example, the widely acclaimed study of S. Dresden, *Persecution, Extermination, Literature* (Toronto 1995). S. Dresden was interned at Westerbork. He has become a well-known author on comparative literature.

5   Source: interview in NRC-Handelsblad 30th of April 1991.

6   Herzberg explains the title of his diary like this: *two directions ran through this camp, and not through this camp alone; National Socialism and Judaism...Two irreconcilable principles here met in invisible combat, though the fatal consequences of that combat were all too apparent.* (Herzberg, 1950:9)

7   He would publish his *Kroniek der Jodenvervolging* in 1950. This widely praised work is much more than a chronicle where he deals with topics which would be discussed much later in an international context like the resistance of the Jews or the 'collaboration' of the Jewish Councils.

8   Among others, Bruno Bettelheim in *Surviving and other Essays* (London,1979) and Michael Pollack in *L'expérience concentrationnaire. Essai sur le maintien de l'identité sociale* (Paris, 1990) discuss writing as a strategy of survival.

9   See: *Uit het werk van dr. J. Presser* (Amsterdam: Atheneum-Polak & Van Gennep, 1969), 195)

10   Renata Laqueur, *Writing in defiance: Concentration Camp Diaries in Dutch, French and German, 1940-1945* (New York, 1971), 156.

11   Like many other diarists, Vogel read a lot and noticed how his literary taste was influenced by his life in Bergen-Belsen. *Thus he seemed to be particularly appreciative of Schopenhauer's dark pessimism, the heroic hedonism of Hemingway, as well as the dry abstractions of scientific psychiatry.* (Laqueur, 1971:174)

Chronology

1889 – 20 April: Adolf Hitler born in Braunau-am-Inn, Austria
       12 May: Otto Frank born in Frankfurt-am-Main, Germany

1919 – 11 November: End of First World War

1929 – *12 June: Anneliese Marie Frank born in Frankfurt-am-Main, Germany. Second child of Otto Frank and Edith Holländer (her sister Margot was born on 16 February 1926)*

1933 – 30 January: Adolf Hitler becomes Chancellor of Germany.
       March: opening of first concentration camp: Dachau
       December: Frank family moves to Amsterdam

1935 – September: Nuremberg racial laws

1938 – 9 November: Kristallnacht

1939 – 1 September: Germany invades Poland: beginning of the Second World War

1940 – 10 May: German invasion of Holland, Belgium and France
       14 May: Bombardment of Rotterdam, next day Holland surrenders

1941 – 25 February: February strike in Amsterdam
       22 June: Hitler invades Russia
       31 July: Goering assigns Heydrich to make all necessary preparations for a *Gesamtlösung der Judenfrage im Deutschen Einflussgebiet in Europa* (Comprehensive Solution of the Jewish Question in German-influenced Europe)
       7 December: Pearl Harbour: America enters the Second World War

1942 – 20 January: Wannsee Conference
       March: Start of Operation Reinhard: mass-gassings begin in three extermination camps: Belzec (March), Sobibor (May) and Treblinka (July); Construction of Auschwitz II (Birkenau)
       Japan occupies the Dutch East Indies
       May: Introduction of Jewish Yellow Star in Holland
       6 July: Frank family goes into hiding – Prinsengracht 263; one week later they are joined by the Van Pels family (in November 1942 a dentist, Fritz Pfeffer, comes to share the hiding-place)
       July: Start of deportations from Westerbork

November: El Alamein, Montgomery defeats the German Afrika Korps under Rommel in North Africa

1943 –   January: Stalingrad, German Sixth Army surrenders
April: Uprising of Warsaw ghetto
November: End of Operation Reinhard

1944 –   6 June: D-Day, Allied Forces invade Normandy
4 August: All eight people at Prinsengracht 263 arrested and taken to Wester-bork
14 September: Battle of Arnhem
3 September: Last train from Westerbork to Auschwitz; Frank family, Van Pels family and Fritz Pfeffer on board
October: Anne and Margot Frank transported from Auschwitz to Bergen-Belsen
December:Battle of the Bulge; Hunger Winter in the west of Holland

1945 –   January-May: Liberation of the concentration camps
7 March: US forces cross the Rhine at Remagen
March: Death of Anne and Margot Frank in Bergen-Belsen
30 April: Adolf Hitler commits suicide in Berlin
6 May: German troops in Holland surrender
8 May: Germany surrenders unconditionally
August: Capitulation of Japan. Proclamation of the Republic of Indonesia

1946 –   The Nuremberg Trials

1947 –   *Publication of* Het Achterhuis, *the diary of Anne Frank*

1948 –   Foundation of the State of Israel

1949 –   After two military campaigns and under pressure from the international community, the Dutch government recognizes the independence of the Republic of Indonesia

1961 –   Eichmann trial in Jerusalem. In the following two decades several trials will take place in Germany against former SS guards of the concentration camps

1980 –   *19 August: Death of Otto Frank*

Short Biographies

Greet van Amstel (1903-1981), born in Amsterdam, belonged to an anarchistic youth movement. In the Twenties she lived with her husband in Berlin where she met, among other artists, Georg Grosz and Kurt Schwitters. After the German invasion of Holland, she immediately joined the resistance, as she did not want to be caught only because she was Jewish. She was deported to Auschwitz. After the war she became well known for her sculptures, her paintings and poems, recollected in *Verboden te leven* (Forbidden to Live).

Elie A. Cohen (1909-1993) neurologist; survived Auschwitz, a number of other camps and the death marches. Much later, he wrote about his experiences in three books: *De afgrond* (The Abyss), *De negentien treinen naar Sobibor* (Nineteen Trains to Sobibor) and *Beelden uit de nacht* (Images of the Night). In 1952, he published his dissertation *Human behaviour in the concentration camp* (New York), one of the first efforts to analyse the psychological defence mechanisms of camp inmates. *The New York Times* of 13 April 1952 called it *a cool, dispassionate inquiry into the mentality of the camps, why the Nazi masters and the prisoners acted as they did.*

Gerard Durlacher (1928-1996), born in Baden-Baden, Germany. He came to Holland in 1936, after his father was offered a job as a sales representative there. In 1942 the family was caught and taken to Westerbork. From there they were transported to Theresienstadt and later to Auschwitz-Birkenau. After the war he returned to Holland and became a lecturer in sociology at the University of Amsterdam. *Stripes in the Sky* was first published in 1985, *Drowning* in 1987, *Quarantaine* in 1993.

Moshe Flinker (1926-1944?), born in The Hague into an Orthodox Jewish family. Fled with his father, mother, five sisters and a brother in November 1942 to Brussels, Belgium. Began to write a diary in Hebrew there. Betrayed by a Jewish informer, the family was arrested on the eve of Pesach 1944 and deported to Auschwitz. All his sisters and his brother survived the camp, Moshe and both his parents were killed. His diary – in Hebrew – was published in 1958, an English edition appeared in 1965, the Dutch translation in 1973.

Anne Frank (1929-1945), born in Frankfurt am Main, Germany, the second child of Otto Frank and Edith Holländer. In 1933 the family moved to Amsterdam in response to the increasing threat of National-Socialism. For her thirteenth birthday (12 June 1942) her father gave her a diary, planning to go into hiding very soon afterwards. During the period of hiding (6 July 1942-4 August 1944) Anne would write almost daily in her diary. On 4 August the eight people in hiding were betrayed and arrested. The diary was saved and kept in a drawer of a desk by Miep Gies, to be given back to Anne on her return. After their arrest the people were taken to Westerbork and left Holland on the 3 September 1944 on the very last train to Auschwitz. From Auschwitz she was transported at the end of October 1944 to Bergen-Belsen, where she died of typhoid fever between 15 and 20 March 1945. Bergen-Belsen was liberated by the British Army on 15th April 1945.

The diary was published after the war by Anne's father, Otto Frank, the only survivor of the eight people who had been in hiding on Prinsengracht 263. First published in 1947, it is now probably the best known book about the fate of the Jews in the Second World War.

Carl Friedman, born in 1952 in Eindhoven. In 1991 she published *Tralievader*. In 1994 it was translated into English and published under the title *Nightfather*. She has also written poems, short stories and essays.

W.F. Hermans (1922-1995), one of Holland's best-known post-war authors. The Second World War played an important role in a number of his novels and plays: *De donkere kamer van Damokles* (1958) (The Dark Room of Damocles), *Herinneringen van een engelbewaarder* (1971) (Memories of a Guardian Angel) and *King Kong* (1972). He was one of the first to see through the lies and prevarications of Friedrich Weinreb.

Abel Herzberg (1893-1989), born in Amsterdam. His parents came from Russia. In *Brieven aan mijn kleinzoon* (Letters to My Grandson) Herzberg told about the ties that bound him to his Russian background, so important for Jewish culture. He became a lawyer and a Zionist. He was deported to Bergen-Belsen during the occupation, where he was a candidate for exchange to Palestine. Liberated in April 1945 near Tröbitz by the Russian army.

Herzberg wrote seven essays about life in Bergen-Belsen, *Amor fati*, shortly after the war. His original diary *Tweestroomenland* (Land of Two Streams) was also published. In 1950 he wrote *Kroniek der jodenvervolging* (Chronicle of the Persecution of the Jews); it belongs, with the works of Presser and De Jong, to the standard works about the persecutions in Holland. Apart from novels, plays and many essays, he published his views on the trial of Eichmann: *Eichmann in Jerusalem* (1962).

Etty Hillesum (1914-1943), born in Middelburg, where her father taught classical languages. Her mother was Russian by birth. Etty studied Law, Slavonic Languages and Psychology in Amsterdam. She befriended Julius Spier, a well-known psychochirologist. For a short while she worked for the Jewish Council of Amsterdam, but soon voluntarily chose to join other Jews in Westerbork. From August 1942 till September 1943 she worked in the hospital there and served as a messenger between Westerbork and Amsterdam. On 7 September 1943 she was put on a 'transport' to Auschwitz, together with her father, mother and brother. She died there on 30 November 1943.

Her diary was first published in 1981 under the title *Het verstoorde leven*, the English translation – *A Disturbed Life – A Diary 1941-1943* – in 1983.

Clarissa Jacobi (ps. for Klara Spits), born in 1920 in Amsterdam. Trained as a ballet dancer. She survived the war by going into hiding, but both her parents died in Sobibor. After the war she emigrated to Cape Town, South Africa, where she has lived ever since. In 1966 she published *Een echte Kavalsky* (A Real Kavalsky) and in 1977, *De waterlanders* (The Waterworks), about her youth in a Jewish family in pre-war Amsterdam.

Louis de Jong, born in Amsterdam in 1914. Studied history at the University of Amsterdam and worked as a journalist. In May 1940 he escaped together with his wife to London, where he became a political commentator with Radio Orange. After his return in 1945 he was appointed director of the Rijksinstituut voor Oorlogsdocumentatie (State Institute for War Documentation). In 1953 his dissertation was published, *The Fifth Column*, translated into many languages. In 1960-65 he broadcast the television documentary *De Bezetting* (The Occupation). Published in 1969-1988 *Het Koninkrijk der Nederlanden in de Tweede Wereldoorlog* (The Kingdom of The Netherlands in the Second World War, 13 parts in 27 volumes; 16,206 pages), still a unique work of encyclopaedic proportions that has no equal in other formerly occupied countries. All aspects of life under occupation are dealt with. The critic of *The Times Literary Supplement* called it 'an unusual combination of qualities'. In 1990 he published his lectures at the University of Harvard under the title *The Netherlands and the Nazi Occupation*.

David Koker (1921-1945), born in Amsterdam. History student before transport to concentration camp Vught in the beginning of 1943, where he began to keep a diary. In June 1944 Koker and his family were deported to Auschwitz. He died before the liberation during a transport from Gross-Rosen to Dachau. In 1977 *Dagboek geschreven in Vught* (Diary Written in Vught) was published.

Renata Laqueur, born in 1919. Daughter of a German emigrant, she went, via Vught and Westerbork, to Bergen-Belsen in the beginning of 1944. In April 1945 she was liberated by the Russians near Tröbitz. Back in Holland she continued her diary. It was published in 1965. She emigrated in 1953 to the USA, and in 1971 the University of New York published her thesis: *Writing in Defiance: Concentration Camp Diaries in Dutch, French and German, 1940-1945*.

Philip Mechanicus (1889-1944), born in Amsterdam. Self-educated as a journalist, he worked as a reporter in the Dutch East Indies and later joined the staff of a daily newspaper *Het Algemeen Handelsblad* as travel editor. The paper fired him in 1940. He was arrested in September 1942 and arrived in Westerbork the following month. There he worked as a nurse in the hospital. He stayed in Westerbork until March 1944, when he was taken to Bergen-Belsen. In October 1944 he was transported from Bergen-Belsen to Auschwitz, where he was presumably shot on 12 October 1944. His accurate account of life in Westerbork, originally called

In Depot, was first published in 1964 – English translation *Waiting for Death* published in 1968.

Marga Minco, born in 1920 in a Jewish family, journalist and one of Holland's leading novelists. Her experiences during the occupation are an important source for many of her novels. In 1957 *Het bittere kruid* (Bitter Herbs) was published, in 1966 *Het lege huis* (An Empty House), in 1983 *De val* (The Fall).

Harry Mulisch, born in 1927 in Haarlem, prolific and famous Dutch novelist. His father being an Austrian and his mother of Jewish descent, he expressed his obsession about the Second World War by saying: 'I am the Second World War'. That obsession is clear from a number of his works: *Het stenen bruidsbed* (The Stone Bridal Bed) from 1959, *De toekomst van gisteren* (The Future of Yesterday), *De zaak 40/61* (on the Eichmann trial) and in 1982 *De Aanslag* (The Assault), a novel that was made into a film, which won an Academy Award as best foreign movie in 1986.

Jona Oberski, born in 1938. Orphaned as a result of the Nazi persecution and himself a survivor of Bergen-Belsen. Published his experiences in 1978 under the title *Kinderjaren* (Childhood). Harold Pinter wrote in his review of the English edition: '...Belsen from the viewpoint of a small boy, Dutch/Jewish. A terrible perspective. The tone of voice never veers away from simple, terse description, but contains a world of bewilderment and agony. Shattering.' *Childhood* has been translated into many languages.

Jacques Presser (1899-1970), born in Amsterdam. Studied history and literature there. Worked as a secondary-school teacher, from 1941 at the German-created Jewish Lyceum. In 1943 his wife – Deborah – was arrested and transported via Westerbork to Sobibor, where she was killed. Presser survived the war in hiding. After the war he was appointed Professor of Modern History at the University of Amsterdam. In 1957 he published the novel *De nacht der Girondijnen* (in 1959 published in English as *Breaking Point*) and in 1965, *Ondergang – De vervolging en verdelging van het Nederlandse Jodendom 1940-1945* (Decline – the Persecution and Destruction of Dutch Jewry), translated into English as *Ashes in the Wind*. Presser died in 1970.

Gerard Reve, born in 1921, famous Dutch novelist. His novella *De ondergang van de familie Boslowits* (The Decline of the Boslowits Family, 1946) established his reputation. Unlike in the works of his two contemporaries, W.F. Hermans and Harry Mulisch, the Second World War hardly features explicitly in his oeuvre, except in his latest book *Het Boek van violet en dood* (The Book of Violet and Death, 1996).

Jules Schelvis, born in 1921 in Amsterdam. Became a printer. Fired in 1941 because of his Jewishness. Caught during the big razzia of May 1943 and taken to Sobibor via Westerbork. The whole transport was gassed on arrival, except a small group of men. He published his memories in 1982 as *Binnen de poorten* (Inside the Gates) and in 1993 an academic study on Sobibor, which received general praise: *Vernietigingskamp Sobibor* (Extermination Camp Sobibor).

Loden Vogel (ps. of Louis M. Tas), born in 1920 in Amsterdam. He came via Vught and Westerbork to Bergen-Belsen. Was liberated by the Russians in April 1945 near Tröbitz. He published his diary notes from Bergen-Belsen shortly after the war. In 1954 he finished his studies in psychology and medicine and became a psychiatrist. In 1965 *Dagboek uit een kamp* (Diary from a Camp) was published with 'self-analysis' as its main motive.

Leo Vroman, born in 1915, studied biology. In May 1940 he escaped to England. When war with Japan broke out, he was drafted and soon became a POW, spending the remaining war years in camps in Java and Japan. After the Japanese surrender, he emigrated to the USA where he started writing poetry in English. He received several Dutch literary awards and American awards for his scientific work. He published more than 65 books, 50 of which are poetry. In 1967 he published a popular non-fiction book, *Blood*.

Grete Weil, born in 1906. With her husband, Edgar Weil, she moved to Amsterdam when the Nazis came to power. There she became a photographer. Her husband was caught during a round-up in 1941 and was murdered in Mauthausen. From 1942 she worked for the Jewish Council (Joodse Raad) and managed, together with another German emigrant, Walter Suskind, to get many people out of the Joodsche Schouwburg (Jewish Theatre). In the autumn of 1943, she went into hiding near the hiding-place of Anne Frank. In 1947 she returned to Bavaria where she has lived ever since. In that year she published her experiences in the Joodsche Schouwburg (Jewish Theatre) in a novel called *Naar het einde van de wereld* (To the End of the World). Much later followed *Tramhalte Beethovenstraat* (Tramstop Beethovenstraat) about the deportations of Jews from the southern part of Amsterdam, and some other novels, including *Happy sagte der Onkel*, three stories taking place in America.

H. Wielek (ps. of Willy Kweksilber) (1912-1988), born in Cologne, Germany. He fled to Holland in 1933 and became one of the most influential 'emigré' writers. His book *De oorlog die Hitler won* (The War That Hitler Won) from 1947 was one of the first attempts to describe 'the suffering from which it was born'.

Jan Wolkers, born in 1925, famous Dutch novelist and sculptor. He designed the Auschwitz Monument in Amsterdam. The Second World War features prominently in his novel *Kort Amerikaans (American Crew Cut*, 1962), which was reprinted many times and turned into a successful movie.

Bibliography

Robert H. Abzug, *Inside the vicious heart. American and the liberation of Nazi concentration camps* (New York 1985)

Jean Améry, *At the mind's limits. Contemplations by a survivor on Auschwitz and its realities* (New York 1990)

Greet van Amstel, *Verboden te leven* (Amsterdam 1965)

Milo Anstadt, *Jonge jaren. Polen – Amsterdam 1920-1940* (Amsterdam 1995)

M.S. Arnoni, *Moeder was niet thuis voor haar begrafenis* (Amsterdam 1984)

Clara Asscher-Pinkhof, *Star children* (Detroit 1987)

Judith Tylor Baumel, *Unfulfilled promise. Rescue and resettlement of Jewish refugee children in the United States 1934-1945* (Juneau 1990)

Michael Berenbaum, *The world must know: the history of the Holocaust as told in the United States Holocaust Memorial Museum* (Boston etc. 1993)

Hetty Berg et al. (eds.), *Geschiedenis van de joden in Nederland* (Amsterdam 1995)

Bericht van de Tweede Wereldoorlog (Amsterdam 1971)

George E. Berkley, *Hitler's gift. The story of Theresienstadt* (Boston 1993)

Michael Andre Bernstein, *Foregone conclusions. Against apocalyptic history* (Berkeley etc. 1994)

Bruno Bettelheim, *The informed heart. The human condition in modern mass society* (London 1961)

Maurice Blanchot, *L'écriture du désastre* (Paris 1986)

Mirjam Blits, *Auschwitz 13917. Hoe ik de Duitse concentratiekampen overleefde* (Amsterdam 1961)

Jacob Boas, *Boulevard des Misères. The story of transit camp Westerbork* (Hamden, Conn. 1985)

Jacob Boas, *We are witnesses. Five diaries of teenagers who died in the Holocaust* (New York 1995)

Corrie ten Boom, *The hiding place* (New York 1974)

Tadeusz Borowski, *This way for the gas, ladies and gentlemen* (London 1976)

Randolph Braham (ed.), *Reflections of the Holocaust in art and literature* (New York 1990)

Chaya Brasz, *Removing the yellow badge. The struggle for a Jewish community in the postwar Netherlands 1944-1955* (Jerusalem 1995)

Philo Bregstein, *Gesprekken met Jacques Presser* (Amsterdam 1972)

Philo Bregstein, *Dingen die niet voorbijgaan. Persoonlijk geschiedverhaal van J. Presser* (Amsterdam 1981)

Alexander Bronowski, *They were few* (New York etc. 1991)

Andreas Burnier, *Het jongensuur* gevolgd door *Oorlog* en *Na de bevrijding* (Amsterdam 1995)

Asher Cohen et al. (eds.), *Comprehending the Holocaust. Historical and literary research* (Frankfurt etc. 1988)

Elie A. Cohen, *Human behaviour in the concentration camp* (New York 1952)

Elie A. Cohen, *De afgrond. Een egodocument* (Amsterdam 1971)

Elie A. Cohen, *De negentien treinen naar Sobibor* (Amsterdam 1979)

Elie A. Cohen, *Beelden uit de nacht. Kampherinneringen* (Amsterdam 1992)

G.J. Colijn and M. Littell (eds.), *The Netherlands and Nazi genocide* (Lewiston N.Y. 1992)

Dagboekfragmenten 1940-1945 (Utrecht 1985)

Bronia Davidson, *Geen tijd voor afscheid* (Amsterdam 1995)

Charlotte Delbo, *None of us will return* (New York 1968)

Charlotte Delbo, *Days and memory* (Marlboro, Vt. 1990)

Ies Dikker, *Nergens veilig. Brief uit de onderduik* (Haarlem 1995)

J.R. Dobschiner, *Selected to live* (London 1969)

S. Dresden, *Literature, persecution, extermination* (Toronto etc. 1995)

Gerard Durlacher, *Drowning. Growing up in the Third Reich* (London/New York 1993)

Gerard Durlacher, *Stripes in the sky* (London/New York 1991)

Gerard Durlacher, *De zoektocht* (Amsterdam 1991)

Gerard Durlacher, *Quarantaine* (Amsterdam 1993)

Debórah Dwork, *Children with a star. Jewish youth in Nazi Europe* (New Haven 1991)

Mandy R. Evans, *Lest we forget* (Berrien Springs Mich. 1991)

Sidra DeKoven Ezrahi, *By words alone. The Holocaust in literature* (Chicago 1980)

Soshana Felman and Dori Laub, *Testimony: crises of witnessing in literature, psychoanalysis and history* (New York etc. 1992)

Ida Fink, *A scrap of time* (London 1988)

Moshe Flinker, *Young Moshe's diary. The spiritual torment of a Jewish boy in Nazi Europe* (Jerusalem 1965)

Eva Fogelman, *Conscience & courage. Rescuers of Jews during the Holocaust* (New York etc. 1994)

Anne Frank, *The diary of Anne Frank: the critical edition* (Amsterdam 1986; New York 1989)

The diary of Anne Frank (London 1995)

Saul Friedlander (ed.), *Probing the limits of representation. Nazism and the Final Solution* (Cambridge Mass. 1992)

Saul Friedlander, *Memory, history, and the extermination of the Jews of Europe* (Bloomington 1993)

Carl Friedman, *Nightfather* (New York 1994)

M.H. Gans, *Memorbook: history of Dutch Jewry from the Renaissance to 1940* (Baarn 1971)

Miep Gies, *Anne Frank remembered* (London 1987)

Martin Gilbert, *The day the war ended. VE-Day 1945 in Europe and around the world* (London 1995)

Arnon Grunberg, *Blue mondays* (New York 1996)

Yisrael Gutman (ed.), *Encyclopedia of the Holocaust* (New York 1990)

Laurel Halliday, *Children in the Holocaust and World War II. Their secret diaries* (New York 1995)

Geoffrey H. Hartman (ed.), *Holocaust remembrance. The shapes of memory* (Cambridge Mass. 1994)

Geoffrey H. Hartman, *The longest shadow. In the aftermath of the Holocaust* (Bloomington 1996)

W.F. Hermans, *The dark room of Damocles* (London 1962)

W.F. Hermans, *Herinneringen van een Engelbewaarder* (Amsterdam 1971)

Abel Herzberg, *Tweestroomenland* (Arnhem 1950)

Abel Herzberg, *Kroniek der Jodenvervolging, 1940-1945* (Amsterdam 1985)

Abel Herzberg, *Amor fati* (Amsterdam 1946, 1965)

Abel Herzberg, *Eichmann in Jeruzalem* (Den Haag 1962)

Abel Herzberg, *Verzameld werk 3* (Amsterdam 1996)

Judith Herzberg, *But what? Selected Poems* (Oberlin Ohio 1988)

Raul Hilberg, *The destruction of the European Jews: revised and definitive edition* (New York 1985)

Raul Hilberg, *Perpretators, victims, bystanders. The Jewish catastrophe 1933-1945* (New York 1992)

Etty Hillesum, *Etty, a diary 1941-1943.* (London 1987; paperback-edition Grafton 1988)

Etty Hillesum, *Letters from Westerbork* (London 1983; paperback-edition 1985)

Etty Hillesum, *An interrupted life. The diaries of Etty Hillesum 1941-43* (London 1983, also: New York 1985)

Herbert Hirsch, *Genocide and the politics of memory. Studying death to preserve life* (Chapell Hill/London 1995)

Gerhard Hirschfeld, *Nazi rule and Dutch collaboration. The Netherlands under German occupation 1940-1945* (Oxford etc. 1988)

Dienke Hondius, *Terugkeer. Antisemitisme in Nederland rond de bevrijding* (Den Haag 1990)

Daniel Johannes Huygens, *Opposite the Lion's Den. A story of hiding Dutch Jews* (Sydney 1996)

Jonathan Israel, *The Dutch Republic. Its rise, greatness and fall 1477-1806* (Oxford 1995)

Clarissa Jacobi, *Een echte Kavalsky* (Amsterdam 1980)

Clarissa Jacobi, *De waterlanders. Een joodse jeugd tussen twee wereldoorlogen* (Baarn 1977)

Volker Jakob en Annet van der Voort, *Anne Frank was niet alleen* (Amsterdam 1990)

Joods Historisch Museum, *Documents of the persecution of the Dutch Jewry 1940-1945* (Amsterdam 1979)

Louis de Jong, *De Bezetting* (Amsterdam 1966)

Louis de Jong, *Herinneringen I* (Den Haag 1993)

Louis de Jong, *The Netherlands and Nazi Germany* (Cambridge Mass. 1990)

Janet Keith, *The incredible story of Arie van Mansum in the Holocaust* (Richmond Hill Ont. 1991)

KL Auschwitz seen by the SS (Oswiecim 1994)

Arthur Koestler, *The Yogi and the Commissar* (London 1985)

David Koker, *Dagboek geschreven in Vught* (Amsterdam 1977)

E.H. Kossman, *The Low Countries 1780-1940* (Oxford 1978)

Dominick LaCapra, *Representing the Holocaust. History, theory, trauma* (Ithaca 1994)

Elaine Landau, *We survived the Holocaust* (New York etc. 1991)

Berel Lang (ed.), *Writing and the Holocaust* (New York etc. 1988)

Renata Laqueur, *Dagboek uit Bergen-Belsen. Maart 1944 – april 1945* (Amsterdam 1965)

Renata Laqueur Weiss, *Writing in defiance. Concentration camp diaries in Dutch, French and German, 1940-1945* (Ann Arbor 1971)

Lawrence L. Langer, *The Holocaust and the literary imagination* (New Haven 1975)

Primo Levi, *The reawakening* (New York 1993)

Primo Levi, *The respite* (s.d, s.l)

Primo Levi, *The truce* (London 1979)

Willy Lindwer, *Kamp van hoop en wanhoop. Getuigen van Westerbork* (Amsterdam 1990)

Willy Lindwer, *The last seven months of Anne Frank* (New York 1991)

Jacqueline van Maarsen, *Anne en Jopie. Leven met Anne Frank* (Amsterdam 1990)

Walter B. Maass, *The Netherlands at war: 1940-1945* (New York 1970)

Geert Mak, *Een kleine geschiedenis van Amsterdam* (Amsterdam 1995)

Philip Mechanicus, *Waiting for death* (London 1968)

Philip Mechanicus, *"Ik woon, zoals je weet, drie hoog." Brieven uit Westerbork* (Amsterdam 1987)

Ischa Meijer, *Brief aan mijn moeder* (Den Haag 1974)

Konrad Merz, *Ein Mensch fällt aus Deutschland* (Frankfurt 1981)

Jozeph Michman (ed.), *Dutch Jewish history. Proceedings of the symposium on the history of the Jews in the Netherlands November 28 – December 3, 1982 Tel Aviv – Jerusalem* (Jerusalem 1984)

Judith Miller, *One, by one, by one. Facing the Holocaust* (New York 1990)

Marga Minco, *Bitter herbs* (London 1960)

Marga Minco, *The glass bridge* (London 1988)

Marga Minco, *An empty house* (London 1990)

Marga Minco, *The fall* (London 1990)

Bob Moore, *Refugees from Nazi Germany in the Netherlands, 1933-1940* (Dordrecht 1986)

Bob Moore, *Victims and survivors. The persecution of the Jews in the Netherlands during the Second World War* (London forthcoming)

Dirk Mulder (ed.), *Westerbork Cahiers* 4 vols.(Assen 1993-1996)

Harry Mulisch, *De Zaak 40/61* (Amsterdam 1963)

Harry Mulisch, *The assault* (London 1986)

Jona Oberski, *Childhood* (London 1983; Toronto 1984)

Samuel P. Oliner and Pearl M., *The altruistic personality – Rescuers of Jews in Nazi Europe* (New York 1988)

Mordecai Paldiel, *The path of the righteous* (New York 1993)

Robert-Jan van Pelt and Debórah Dwork, *Auschwitz. 1270 to the present* (London 1996)

Frans Pointl, *Ongeluk is ook een soort geluk* (Amsterdam 1995)

Jacob Presser, *Breaking point* (Cleveland 1958, recently published under the title: *The night of the Girondists*, London 1992)

Jacob Presser, *The destruction of the Dutch Jews* (New York 1969, reprint: Detroit 1988)

Mirjam Pressler, *Daar verlang ik zo naar* (Amsterdam 1993)

Johanna Reiss, *The upstairs room* (New York 1972, 1980)

Johanna Reiss, *The journey back* (Oxford 1977)

Gerard Reve, *The destruction of the Boslowits Family* (London 1973)

Ruud van der Rol and Rian Verhoeven, *Anne Frank: beyond the diary. A photographic remembrance* (Amsterdam 1992; New York 1993)

Leesha Rose, *The tulips are red* (South Brunswick etc. 1978)

Alvin H. Rosenfeld, *A double dying. Reflections on Holocaust literature* (Bloomington 1980)

Abram L. Sachar, *The redemption of the unwanted* (New York 1983)

Simon Schama, *The embarrassment of riches. An interpretation of Dutch culture in the Golden Age* (New York 1987)

Jules Schelvis, *Binnen de poorten* (Amsterdam 1982)

Jules Schelvis, *Vernietigingskamp Sobibor* (Amsterdam 1993)

Eva Schloss, *Eva's story. A survivor's tale by the step-sister of Anne Frank* (London 1988)

Ernst Schnabel, *The footsteps of Anne Frank* (London 1961)

Fred Schwarz, *Treinen op dood spoor* (Amsterdam 1994)

Eric Silver, *The book of the just. The silent heroes who saved Jews from Hitler* (London 1992)

Johan M. Snoek, *The grey book. A collection of protests against antisemitism and the persecution of Jews by non-roman catholic churches and church leaders during Hitler's rule* (Assen 1969)

Barry Spanjaard, *Don't fence me in. An American teenager in the Holocaust* (Saugus Cal. 1981)

Julian Castle Stanford, *Reflections. The diary of a German-Jew in hiding* (Oakland Cal. 1965)

André Stein, *Quiet heroes: true stories of the rescue of the Jews by Christians in Nazi-occupied Holland* (New York 1988)

Studia Rosenthaliana, special issue, proceedings of the 5th international symposium on the history of the Jews in the Netherlands, edited by M.P. Beukers en J.J. Cahen (Assen 1989)

Tzvetan Todorov, *Facing the extreme. Moral life in the concentration camps* (New York 1996)

Barry Turner, *...and the policemen smiled. 10.000 children escape from Nazi Europe* (London 1990)

Hilde Verdoner-Sluizer, *Signs of life* (Washington D.C. 1990)

Loden Vogel, *Dagboek uit een kamp* (Amsterdam 1965)

Ida Vos, *Hide and seek* (Boston 1991)

S. de Vries Jr., *Verduisterde jaren* (Amsterdam 1945)

Esther van Vriesland, *Esther. Een dagboek 1942* (Utrecht 1990)

Leo Vroman, *De adem van Mars* (Amsterdam 1956)

Werner Warmbrunn, *The Dutch under German occupation, 1940-1945* (Stanford Cal. 1963)

Grete Weil, *Tramhalte Beethovenstraat* (Wiesbaden 1963)

Grete Weil, *Ans Ende der Welt* (Frankfurt 1989)

H. Wielek, *De oorlog die Hitler won* (Amsterdam 1947)

Suzette Wyers, *Als ik wil kan ik duiken...Brieven van Claartje van Aals* (Amsterdam 1995)

Rolf Wolfswinkel, *Tussen landverraad en vaderlandsliefde. De collaboratie in naoorlogs proza* (Amsterdam 1994)

Jan Wolkers, *Kort Amerikaans* (Amsterdam 1962)

James E. Young, *Writing and rewriting the Holocaust. Narrative and the consequences of interpretation* (Bloomington 1988)

Nanda van der Zee, *De kamergenoot van Anne Frank* (Amsterdam 1990)

Sources

Translations of texts cited in this book were originally published by:

Boas, Jacob: Holt, New York.
Dresden, Sem: Toronto UP, Toronto.
Durlacher, Gerard: Serpent's Tail, London/New York.
Flinker, Moshe: Yad Vashem, Jerusalem.
Frank, Anne: Netherlands State Institute for War Documentation, Amsterdam.
The diary of Anne Frank: Macmillan, London.
Friedman, Carl: Persea Books, New York.
Gies, Miep: Transworld Publishers, London.
Gilbert, Martin: Harper Collins, London.
Herzberg, Judith: Oberlin College Press, Oberlin Ohio.
Hillesum, Etty: Jonathan Cape, London.
Jong, Louis de: Harvard UP, Cambridge Mass.
Lindwer, Willy: Pantheon Books, New York.
Mechanicus, Philip: Coldar and Boyars, London.
Minco, Marga: Oxford University Press, London; Owen, London.
Mulisch, Harry: Penguin, London.
Oberski, Jona: Hodder and Stoughton, London; Lester & Orpen Dennys, Toronto.
Presser, Jacob: World Pub, Cleveland; Harvill, London, and Dutton, New York.
Schloss, Eva: W.H. Allen, London.

The photographs reproduced in this book all originate from the Netherlands State Institute for War Documentation, except those on p. 67 (below) (© Joh. de Haas, Amsterdam), p. 61 (© L. van Nobelen, Amsterdam), p. 69 (© A. Wijnberg, Amsterdam) and p. 119 (© Anne Frank Stichting, Amsterdam).

Index

Aals, Claartje 64
Abzug, Robert 125
Adorno, Theodor 149
Amerongen-Frankfoorder, Rachel
  van 89, 118
Améry, Jean 150
Amstel, Greet van 124, 128, 149,
  161, 169
Anstadt, Milo 25
Arendt, Hannah 133, 148
Arnoni, Menachem 106, 145, 159
Asscher, Abraham 40, 98, 132
Auden, W.H. 28

Bach, J.S. 22
Bauer, Yehuda 160
Beatrix, Queen 122
Beauvoir, Simone de 122
Begley, Louis 147
Bellow, Saul 137
Bettelheim, Bruno 65, 66, 131, 163
Blanchot, Maurice 149
Blits, Mirjam 96, 105, 107, 151
Blom, J.C.H. 157
Boas, Jacob 157
Borowski, Tadeusz 104, 150
Braak, Menno ter 25, 156
Brandes-Brilleslijper, Janny 89, 101,
  115, 116, 141, 143
Braun, Eva 121
Breitman, Richard 161
Burnier, Andreas 66, 126
Busch, Ernst 28

Capitein, Jacobus 16
Christiansen, Friedrich 59
Churchill, Winston 111, 160
Cleveringa, 36
Cohen, David 40, 41, 100
Cohen, Elie 48, 59, 81, 95, 98, 104,
  106, 112, 132, 136, 157, 162

Cohen, Herman 41

Daan, van 158
Davidson, Bronia 129
Delbo, Charlotte 124, 150
Descartes, René 16
Dijk, Ans van 132
Dikker, Ies 46, 122
Dimbleby, Richard 124
Dresden, Sem 145, 163
Durlacher, Gerard 12, 23, 25, 26, 98,
  103, 106, 107, 111, 126, 127, 133,
  135, 147, 150, 169
Dussel, Albert 144, 158
Dwork, Debórah 159

Edelstein, Jacob 99
Eden, Anthony 110, 111
Ehrlich, Max 85
Eichmann, Adolf 10, 71, 53, 55, 91,
  93, 124, 133, 134, 166, 170, 172
Eisler, Hans 28
Eliot, T.S. 21
Etty, Esther 81

Felman, Shoshana 148
Flinker, Moshe 48, 59, 68, 82, 110,
  153, 169
Fokkens, M. 17
Frank, Anne (Anneliese Marie) 13-
  14, 31, 48, 50-51, 55, 58, 65, 72-73,
  101, 115-117, 122, 135, 140-145,
  151, 153, 161, 165-166, 169-170,
  173
Frank, Edith 31, 72, 116
Frank, family 23, 65, 89, 115, 118,
  102, 166
Frank, Margot 31, 50-51, 55, 72, 115-
  117, 140, 143, 165-166

Frank, Otto   30-31, 51, 64-65, 72-73,
    115, 140-142, 161-162, 165-166,
    169-170
Friedlander, Henry   160
Friedlander, Saul   148
Friedman, Carl   138, 170
Fünten, Ferdinand aus der   43, 63,
    76, 135
Fussell, Paul   21

Gans, Mozes   136
Geiringer, Eva   143
Gemmeker, Konrad   78, 84, 149
Gerron, Kurt   100
Gies, Jan   140-142
Gies, Miep   50, 51, 64, 72, 73, 140-
    142, 158, 170
Gilbert, Martin   160
Goering, Hermann   43, 45, 165
Goldhagen, Daniel   160
Goldstein-van Cleef, Ronnie   102,
    116
Goodrich, Frances   141, 162
Goschlar, Hanne(li)   143
Goslar, Hannah   31, 50, 117, 141
Gréco, Juliette   122
Griffioen, Pim   157
Grosz, George   169
Grunberg, Arnon   138

Hackett, Albert   141, 162
Harster, Wilhelm   55
Heine, Heinrich   20
Hermans, W.F.   34, 159, 170, 172
Herzberg, Abel   10, 23, 36, 46, 68, 78-
    79, 83, 94-96, 113, 130, 133-134,
    151, 160, 163, 170
Herzberg, Judith   42, 130, 150, 153,
    156
Heydrich, Reinhard   43, 53-54, 165
Hillesum, Etty   57, 78, 81-81, 84-85,
    111, 153, 170
Hillesum, Jaap   81
Hillesum, Mischa   81, 83
Himmler, Heinrich   54, 100, 104, 112
Hitchcock, Alfred   124, 159
Hitler, Adolf   9, 22-23, 28-30, 34, 54,
    121, 136, 157, 160, 165
Hoess, Hedwig   160
Hoess, Rudolf   104

Holländer, Edith   165, 169
Huizinga, Johan   16, 18, 156

Jacobi, Clarissa (= ps. of Clara
    Spits)   34, 108, 171
Jong, Louis (Loe) de   10-11, 23, 35,
    68, 105-106, 133, 148, 151, 156,
    170-171

Kafka, Franz   162
Kaletta, Charlotte   144
Karski, Jan   110, 160
Kertész, Imre   148
Kiš, Danilo   151
Kniesmeijer, Joke   144
Koestler, Arthur   11, 111
Kofman, Sarah   150
Koker, David   87-88, 91, 94, 152-153,
    171
Kraay, Suzy   60
Kramer, Josef   96
Krell, Robert   121
Kweksilber, Willy (= ps. of H. Wie-
    lek)   34, 156, 173

Lages, Willy   135, 162
Lanzmann, Claude   135, 148
Laqueur, Renata   93-95, 113, 127,
    152-153, 160-161, 163, 171
Lederman, Susanne (Sanne)   31, 143
Lehmann, Kurt: see Merz, Konrad
Levi, Primo   107, 124, 126, 148, 150-
    151, 161
Levisson, Bob   111
Lindwer, Willy   89, 101, 135, 143

Maarsen, Jacqueline van   143
Macmillan, Mamice Harold   156
Mahler, Gustav   45
Malamud, Bernard   137
Mann, Erika   28
Mann, Thomas   28
Margry, K.   159
Mayer-Roos, Anita   143
Mechanicus, Philip   77-78, 81, 84-85,
    93, 98, 152-153, 157, 171
Meijer, Ischa   137, 162
Meijer, Jaap   49, 113, 136-138
Mendelssohn, Moses   45
Mengele, Dr. Josef   106-107

Merz, Konrad (=ps. of Kurt Leh-
  mann) 22, 28
Meyer Levin 162
Michel 109
Michman, Dan 156
Minco, Marga 12, 23, 49, 131-132,
  137, 172
Mok, Maurits 109, 112, 136
Mulisch, Harry 70, 134-135, 172

Nolte, Ernst 149

Oberski, Jona 12, 57, 94, 130, 138,
  147, 172
Orange, William III of 18

Patton, George, S. 125
Pels, Augusta van 72
Pels, family van 72, 89, 165-166
Pelt, Robert-Jan van 159
Perkins, Millie 141
Pfeffer, Dr. Fritz 72, 89, 144, 158,
  165-166
Pinter, Harold 172
Pinto, David de 18
Pointl, Frans 137
Pollack, Michael 163
Presser, Deborah (Dé) 11, 161, 172
Presser, Jacques 9-11, 23, 56, 58, 71,
  77, 84, 107, 134, 137-138, 149, 152,
  156-157, 161, 172
Pressler, Mirjam 144

Randwijk, Henk van 69
Rauter, Hanns Albin 55, 157
Reve, Gerard 62, 172
Reynolds, Quentin 157
Richmond, Theo 149
Riegner, Gerhard 110
Rol, Ruud van der 144
Romein, Jan 141
Roosevelt, Franklin Delano 110-111
Rosen, Willy 28, 85
Rosenberg, Alfred 45
Roth, Philip 137

Saint Saëns 45, 57
Santrouschitz, Hermine 142
Sartre, Jean-Paul 122
Schelvis, Jules 105, 109, 172

Schlesinger, Kurt 84
Schloss, Eva 102, 106, 143, 161
Schnabel, Ernst 141
Schuschu (= ps. of Joachim Simon)
  60
Schwarz, Fred 99
Schwitters, Kurt 169
Seyss-Inquart, Arthur 35, 43, 55, 58,
  132, 157, 161
Silberbauer, Karl 73
Simon, Joachim: see Schuschu
Slottke, Fräulein Gertrud 96
Spier, Jo 100
Spier, Julius 170
Spinoza, Baruch de 16
Spits, Clara: see Clarissa Jacobi
Steiner, George 148
Stevens, George 141
Suskind, Walter 173

T. Cornelia 121
Tas, Louis M. 173
Tisma, Alexander 163
Todorov, Tzvetan 160
Truman, Harry 125

Verhoeven, Rian 144
Vian, Boris 122
Visser, L.E. 37, 40, 49
Vogel, Loden 93-96, 113, 152-153,
  163, 173
Vries Jr., S. de 45, 69, 122
Vriesland, Esther van 48
Vroman, Leo 34, 173

Waal, Jopie de 143
Wallenberg, Raoul 160
Weidner, Jean 59-60
Weidner, Gabrielle 60
Weil, Grete 60, 173
Weil, Edgar 173
Weinreb, Friedrich 56, 134, 170
Weismuller, Truus 34
Wells, H.G. 110
Westerweel, Joop 60
Wielek, H.: see Willy Kweksilber
Wiesel, Elie 148, 151
Wiesenthal, Simon 135
Wijsmuller, Truus 28
Wilhelmina, Queen 34, 76

Wolkers, Jan 66, 173

Zee, Nanda van der 144
Zeller, Ron 157

Ziegler, Erich 85
Zöpf, Wilhelm 55
Zygielbojm, Szmul 111